KU-637-256

Thomas Cook

HOTSPOTS

JERSEY

Written by Lindsay Hunt, updated by Anwer Bati

Published by Thomas Cook Publishing
A division of Thomas Cook Tour Operations Limited.
Company registration no. 1450464 England
The Thomas Cook Business Park, Unit 9, Coningsby Road,
Peterborough PE3 8SB, United Kingdom
Email: books@thomascook.com, Tel: + 44 (0) 1733 416477
www.thomascookpublishing.com

Produced by Cambridge Publishing Management Limited
Burr Elm Court, Main Street, Caldecote CB23 7NU

ISBN: 978-1-84157-910-8

First edition © 2006 Thomas Cook Publishing
This second edition © 2008
Text © Thomas Cook Publishing,
Maps © Thomas Cook Publishing/PCGraphics (UK) Limited

Series Editor: Diane Ashmore
Production/DTP: Steven Collins

Printed and bound in Spain by GraphyCems

Front cover photography © SIME/Giovanni Simeone

All rights reserved. No part of this publication may be reproduced, stored in
a retrieval system or transmitted, in any form or by any means, electronic,
mechanical, recording or otherwise, in any part of the world, without prior
permission of the publisher. Requests for permission should be made to the
publisher at the above address.

Although every care has been taken in compiling this publication, and the contents
are believed to be correct at the time of printing, Thomas Cook Tour Operations
Limited cannot accept any responsibility for errors or omission, however caused,
or for changes in details given in the guidebook, or for the consequences of any
reliance on the information provided. Descriptions and assessments are based on
the author's views and experiences when writing and do not necessarily represent
those of Thomas Cook Tour Operations Limited.

CONTENTS

INTRODUCTION............................5
Getting to know Jersey 8
The best of Jersey 14
Symbols key.......................................16

RESORTS 17
St Helier 18
St Clement & Grouville................24
St Martin & Trinity.......................28
St John & St Mary..........................33
St Ouen 37
St Peter & St Brelade 41
St Lawrence & St Saviour 46

EXCURSIONS 49
Beach tour...50
North coast drive............................54
St Peter Port, Guernsey..............59
Northern Guernsey.......................64
South-west Guernsey...................67
South-east Guernsey....................71
Alderney...76
Herm..82
Sark...87

LIFESTYLE 95
Food & drink....................................96
Shopping...100
Children..102
Festivals & events 104
Sports & activities 106

PRACTICAL INFORMATION....109
Accommodation 110
Preparing to go...............................112
During your stay..............................117

INDEX 125

MAPS
Jersey 6
St Helier 19
Guernsey...60
St Peter Port.......................................62
Alderney..77
Herm...83
Sark 88

WHAT'S IN YOUR GUIDEBOOK?

Independent authors Impartial, up-to-date information from our travel experts who meticulously source local knowledge.

Experience Thomas Cook's 165 years in the travel industry and guidebook publishing enriches every word with expertise you can trust.

Travel know-how Contributions by thousands of staff around the globe, each one living and breathing travel.

Editors Travel-publishing professionals, pulling everything together to craft a perfect blend of words, pictures, maps and design.

You, the traveller We deliver a practical, no-nonsense approach to information, geared to how you really use it.

● *St Aubin harbour*

INTRODUCTION
Getting to know Jersey

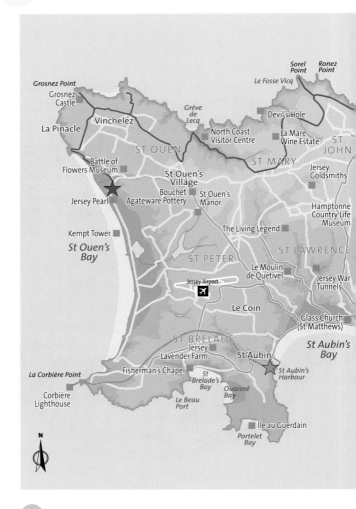

Grosnez Point
Grosnez Castle
La Pinacle
Vinchelez
Grève de Lecq
Sorel Point
Ronez Point
Le Fosse Vicq
Devil's Hole
North Coast Visitor Centre
La Mare Wine Estate
ST JOHN
Battle of Flowers Museum
ST OUEN
St Ouen's Village
Jersey Goldsmiths
Jersey Pearl
Bouchet Agateware Pottery
St Ouen's Manor
ST MARY
Hamptonne Country Life Museum
Kempt Tower
The Living Legend
St Ouen's Bay
ST PETER
ST LAWRENCE
Le Moulin de Quételel
Jersey War Tunnels
Jersey Airport
Le Coin
Glass Church (St Matthews)
ST BRELADE
Jersey Lavender Farm
St Aubin
St Aubin's Bay
La Corbière Point
Fisherman's Chapel
St Brelade's Bay
St Aubin's Harbour
Corbière Lighthouse
Le Beau Port
Ouaisné Bay
Île au Guerdain
Portelet Bay
N

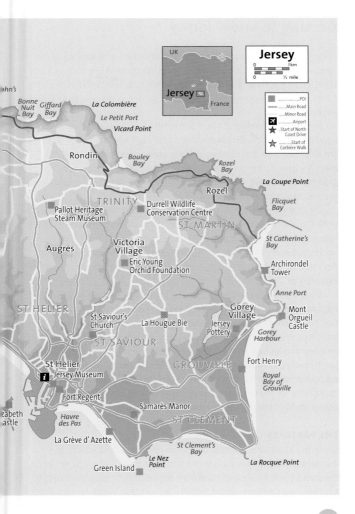

UK

Jersey

France

Jersey

0   1 km

0   ½ mile

POI
Main Road
Minor Road
Airport
Start of North
Coast Drive
Start of
Corbière Walk

hn's

Bonne
Nuit
Bay

Giffard
Bay

La Colombière

Le Petit Port

Vicard Point

Rondin

Bouley
Bay

Rozel
Bay

La Coupe Point

Rozel

Flicquet
Bay

TRINITY   Durrell Wildlife
Conservation Centre

Pallot Heritage
Steam Museum

ST MARTIN

St Catherine's
Bay

Augres

Victoria
Village

Eric Young
Orchid Foundation

Archirondel
Tower

Anne Port

ST HELIER

St Saviour's
Church

La Hougue Bie

Gorey
Village

Jersey
Pottery

Mont
Orgueil
Castle

ST SAVIOUR

Gorey
Harbour

GROUVILLE

Fort Henry

St Helier

Jersey Museum

Fort Regent

Royal
Bay of
Grouville

zabeth
astle

Havre
des Pas

Samarès Manor

ST CLEMENT

La Grève d'Azette

St Clement's
Bay

Le Nez
Point

Green Island

La Rocque Point

Getting to know Jersey

Feeling soft sand between your toes and hearing waves lapping gently against the rocks, it is hard to remember that somewhere there is a fast lane. Jersey is an island where the cars seem to amble through the leafy lanes as in some bygone age. Life doesn't get more peaceful than Jersey – rush hour aside!

Jersey lies in the Bay of Mont St Michel and is the largest and southernmost of the Channel Islands. Although part of the British Isles, the Channel Islands are geographically much closer to France than to the UK – lying 20 km (14 miles) from the coast of Normandy, but 160 km (100 miles) from the south coast of England. The climate is a good deal warmer and sunnier than in the UK.

On a European scale, Jersey seems minute, but size isn't everything. In fact, the small scale of this seductive island is part of its charm. Jersey is only around 15 km (9 miles) at its widest point and 8 km (5 miles) across, but every inch of its surface basks in southerly sunshine for the best part of the year, although it isn't immune from high winds and the odd shower.

Most visitors to the island arrive by plane or by fast ferry from Poole, Portsmouth and Weymouth in England, or from St Malo in France. The first things they notice are the idyllic quaintness of the waterfront buildings, the green of the gentle hills beyond, the sheer size of the beaches and its rugged coastline. Jersey experiences tides of up to 12 m (40 ft) every day, making it one of only a few places in the world with such extreme tidal conditions. The result is that its coastline changes constantly. For the energetic it is possible to walk over 3 km (2 miles) out seawards from the high-water mark on an extreme tide!

THE PARISHES

Jersey has 12 parishes, almost all enjoying their own little bit of the dramatic coastline. The main resort and the 'city' of Jersey is St Helier on the south coast. However, St Brelade's Bay boasts of being the most southerly seaside town in the British Isles – a claim which is only

🔺 *The famous Jersey cows, prized for their creamy milk*

occasionally challenged by St Helier. Some of the best beaches can be found along the south and eastern coast areas of St Clement and Grouville, although St Ouen, St Peter and St Brelade to the west also have their share. Along the north coast there are some beautiful little coves to explore: head for the parishes of St Martin, Trinity, St John and St Mary and look out for the signs to places such as Rozel Bay, Bonne Nuit Bay and Grève de Lecq. Two of the parishes, St Lawrence and St Saviour, are typified by their great expanses of open countryside, where some of Jersey's prettiest wild flowers can be seen.

1066 AND ALL THAT...

The French call the Channel Islands 'Les Îles Anglo-Normandes'. They once formed part of the Duchy of Normandy, and passed into English hands with William the Conqueror. When King John lost control of his

🔺 *The busy harbour at St Aubin*

Norman possessions in 1204, the Channel Islanders were given the choice of reverting to France or remaining English. Shrewdly, they opted for the English side, on condition that they retained their own government and their ancient feudal privileges, relics of which they still hold today.

Thus the Channel Islands are within the British Isles, but they are not part of the United Kingdom – although you'll see the Union Flag widely flown around the island. They have their own government and culture, their own laws and customs – even their own currency, postal services and tax systems. They bear allegiance to the Crown, but not to Westminster. Nor do they bear allegiance to Brussels – the Channel Islands are not full members of the EU. For the Channel Islanders, the British monarch is still the Duke of Normandy, and when they drink a loyal toast, they raise their glasses to 'The Queen, Our Duke'. A dialect of Norman French, *Jèrraise*, is still spoken on the island, although not widely.

It is important to note that age-old rivalries still exist between the islanders, especially Jersey and Guernsey, who took separate sides in the English Civil War (1642).

SEIGNEURS & DAMES

The feudal system imposed by the Normans, in which parcels of land were granted by the king in exchange for military service, has long since lapsed on the larger islands. But some of the ancient manor houses remain, a few of which are still inhabited by descendants of the original seigneurial families. St Ouen's Manor (see map on page 6) is one.

North-east of Jersey, its nearest island neighbour, Sark, tantalised political historians as the last remaining feudal society in Europe, with its Seigneur or Dame as ruler, in name if not in practice. By one of those odd paradoxes so typical of the Channel Islands, however, it was never actually feudal during feudal times. Its seigneurial system dates only from 1565. But in 2006, Sark voted for democracy, with 28 elected representatives (out of a population of around 600), although the Seigneur still has a titular role.

ROYAL MISTRESS

Lillie Langtry was the talk of the islands in the late 19th century. Born in St Saviour's parish in 1853, daughter of the Dean of Jersey, she became a celebrated society beauty. She was also an exceptionally vivacious and intelligent woman who founded her own acting company and toured around in her own train. This in itself was scandalous enough at the time, but Lillie achieved particular notoriety as an acknowledged mistress of the Prince of Wales, later Edward VII.

You can find out more about Lillie in the Jersey Museum, where you can see her ornate travelling case and a gorgeous portrait, *The Jersey Lily*, by Sir John Millais. Lillie was christened, married (twice) and buried in St Saviour's Church. Her marble monument is signposted in the churchyard.

🔺 *One of Jersey's lovely beaches*

WORLD WAR II

World War II is an unforgettable period in Jersey's history as it, along with its neighbouring islands, was the only part of the British Isles to be invaded by the Germans. The Occupation story is told in many museums all over the islands, and visitors often find them fascinating. Don't forget to look at the liberation monuments, too. You'll find Jersey's exuberant bronze sculpture of flag-waving revellers in Liberation Square. The best places to find out more are:

- **Occupation Tapestry** This impressive work tells the story of the island of Jersey during World War II and is the island's largest ever community project (see page 21).
- **Jersey War Tunnels** This dark complex of tunnels is one of the most chilling reminders of the German Occupation period on any of the Channel Islands (see page 48).

JERSEY TODAY

Low taxation makes Jersey and its neighbouring islands extremely attractive for wealthy settlers; there is always a long queue of millionaires on the waiting list. For holiday visitors, though, the lower costs of some items, especially jewellery, alcohol, car hire and petrol, give Jersey that extra sparkle.

Partly because of its tax status, Jersey is a wealthy place, and its residents enjoy the good life in smart restaurants and yacht marinas, with the town of St Helier at its heart. Haute couture, fine jewels and expensive perfumes vie for the attention of shoppers keen for a tax-free bargain.

But Jersey is changing, and trying to alter its image. In the past, most visitors were families, or older people (the average age of tourists at the time of writing is 57), staying for a week or longer. But after recent major investment in infrastructure, accommodation and attractions, the aim is to turn the island into an upmarket short break destination that also appeals to younger people.

THE BEST OF JERSEY

Whether you like beautiful landscapes and coast, traditional crafts, history, family fun, shopping, or just eating and drinking, Jersey has the lot.

TOP 10 ATTRACTIONS

- **Beaches** Jersey has gorgeous beaches, some with huge swathes of sand, some that are great for rock-pooling, and others that are prized for surfing and sailing (see pages 50–53).

- **Jersey War Tunnels** A unique and vast complex of tunnels that once housed the World War II German military hospital, now a moving Occupation museum (see page 48).

- **Samarès Manor** This lovely house, with its alluring gardens, is a must for many visitors (see page 26).

- **Hamptonne Country Life Museum** This fascinating farm museum transports you to the past, and the way life was lived on Jersey (see page 47).

- **Gorey Harbour and Mont Orgueil Castle** Perhaps the island's prettiest harbour, with a recently renovated fortress (see page 30).

- **Churches** Three of Jersey's most interesting parish churches are: St Matthew's, famous for its white glasswork by René Lalique (see page 46); St Brelade's, and its Fishermen's Chapel (see page 43); and St Saviour's, where Lillie Langtry was born, married and buried (see pages 12 and 46).

- **Jersey Museum** Presents the island's colourful history from prehistoric to recent times (see page 20).

- **Elizabeth Castle** Built on two islets near St Helier, it defended Jersey from the 17th century onwards (see page 18).

- **Durrell Wildlife Conservation Trust** Jersey's famous zoo now concentrates on education and conservation (see page 28).

- **Pottering round the country lanes** Whether by car, bike or on foot, take a map and explore Jersey's pretty lanes (see pages 54–8).

◗ *The beautiful herb garden at Samarès Manor*

SYMBOLS KEY
The following symbols are used throughout this book:

ⓐ address ☏ telephone ⓦ website address
🕒 opening times ❶ important

The following symbols are used on the maps:

𝒊	information office	◯	city
✉	post office	◯	large town
✈	airport	○	small town
✚	hospital	▩	POI (point of interest)
🛡	police station	—	main road
🚌	bus station	—	minor road
✝	church	—	railway
❶	numbers denote featured cafés, restaurants & evening venues		

RESTAURANT CATEGORIES
The symbol after the name of each restaurant listed in this guide indicates the price of a typical three-course meal without drinks for one person:
£ = under £25   ££ = £25–45   £££ = over £45

▶ *Mont Orgueil Castle, Gorey*

RESORTS
Places under the sun

RESORTS

St Helier

St Helier's waterfront, formerly a dreary area of commercial wharfs and ferry terminals dominated by a power station, continues to undergo a massive refurbishment. There are many new public spaces, fountains and facilities being created. The attractive buildings housing the **Occupation Tapestry** and **Maritime Museum** are a good start. Across the sweeping, sheltered bay of St Aubin is **Elizabeth Castle**, a Tudor fortress, romantically floodlit at night.

Liberation Square, focus of post-World War II jubilation, makes a natural starting point. Nearby is the colourful **Steam Clock**. In the streets behind you'll discover the town's true character – quaint old shop-fronts and names in Norman French. Visit the delightful old market and historic **Royal Square**, where one of the Commonwealth's oldest parliaments sits. The immaculate gardens of **Howard Davis Park** offer a peaceful retreat.

Several of Jersey's best museums, run by the Jersey Heritage Trust, have a combined ticketing scheme – excellent value if you visit more than a couple. Season tickets allow unlimited visits.

THINGS TO SEE & DO

Elizabeth Castle

The unmissable causeway fortress in St Aubin's Bay dates from the 1590s, and was named after Elizabeth I. History exhibitions and the Royal Jersey Militia Museum are inside. Access is on foot (low tide only) or by an amphibious vehicle dubbed the 'duck' (extra charge). Behind the castle is the Hermitage, a 12th-century chapel dedicated to St Helier, who was murdered by axe-wielding pirates.

ⓐ St Aubin's Bay ❶ 01534 723971 ❷ 10.00–18.00 (mid-Mar–Oct)
❶ Admission charge; difficult access for visitors with disabilities

Fort Regent

The curious golf-ball structure towering over St Helier's harbour houses a massive sports, leisure and entertainment complex in the grounds of a

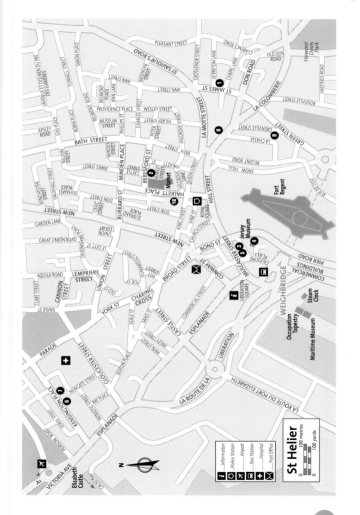

St Helier

19th-century fort. It also has a 2,000-seat concert hall. Learn the history of the fort on a guided tour, and don't miss the signalling tower and the rampart views.

ⓐ Harbour ⓣ 01534 449600 ⓛ Opening times vary according to activity or event ⓘ Admission free, pay as you play

Jersey Museum

An award-winning multi-media presentation of Jersey's history and culture, with an art gallery and excellent catering facilities. Interesting sections on Lillie Langtry (Edward VII's glamorous mistress), and a restored merchant's house on the top floor.

ⓐ The Weighbridge ⓣ 01534 633300 ⓛ 10.00–17.00 (Apr–Oct); 10.00–16.00 (winter) ⓘ Admission charge

Maritime Museum

In the same attractive, waterfront premises as the Occupation Tapestry (see opposite), this excellent museum has many entertaining 'hands-on'

⬤ *A visit to Elizabeth Castle is a must*

ways to learn about tides, winds, cleats and sails. A must for sailing enthusiasts.

ⓐ New North Quay ☎ 01534 811043 🕐 10.00–17.00 (Apr–Oct); 10.00–16.00 (winter) ❶ Admission charge

Occupation Tapestry

The Occupation Tapestry was an ambitious project to commemorate the 50th anniversary of the Liberation in 1995. The whole island was involved, with each parish contributing one of the dozen panels depicting Jersey's wartime experiences. Displayed in a quayside warehouse, the tapestry contains over seven million stitches. Informative video and gift shop.

ⓐ New North Quay ☎ 01534 811043 🕐 10.00–17.00 (Apr–Oct); 10.00–16.00 (Nov–Mar) ❶ Admission charge

TAKING A BREAK

As you might expect, St Helier has the widest choice of eating and drinking places on the island, including large and reliable chain restaurants, such as Pizza Express and McDonald's. Several pubs offer regular live music in the evenings.

The Admiral Wine & Ale House £ ❶ One of St Helier's best-known haunts for inexpensive lunchtime food, decent bitter and dominoes.
ⓐ St James Street ☎ 01534 730095 🕐 12.00–14.00, 18.00–20.15 Mon–Thur; lunch only Fri–Sun 12.00–15.00

Atlantique Seafood Bar £ ❷ In the fish market, in the centre of town, this is a must if you like fresh seafood. ⓐ Beresford Market ☎ 01534 720052 🕐 11.30–15.00 Mon–Sat, 18.30–21.00 Thur–Sat

Chambers £ ❸ A younger sibling of the long-established Admiral, this popular pub appeals to a lively crowd, with regular music in the evenings. It has well-kept beers and good-value bar food. ⓐ Mulcaster Street ☎ 01534 735405 🕐 12.00–15.00 daily & 18.00–21.00 Mon–Thur

Jersey Museum Brasserie £ ❹ This excellent brasserie is open to non-museum visitors and serves sophisticated snacks and cakes. ⓐ Weighbridge ❶ 01534 510069 ⊙ Museum hours and for evening dining from 18.30

AFTER DARK

Restaurants & pubs

Café Zephyr ££ ❺ The café (there are also two other good restaurants) at the Royal Yacht hotel is about the trendiest place to eat on the island. Contemporary food with Asian and Italian influences. ⓐ Weighbridge ❶ 01534 720511 ⓦ www.theroyalyacht.com ⊙ 09.00–22.00 Mon–Thur, 07.00–22.00 Fri–Sun

Candlelight Restaurant ££ ❻ This restaurant serves French and English cuisine and fine wines in traditional surroundings. Part of the Revere Hotel, a 17th-century coach house, and within walking distance of the Esplanade. ⓐ Kensington Place ❶ 01534 611111 ⊙ 18.45–21.00

Doran's Courtyard Bistro ££ ❼ An intimate ambience of warehouse windows, rustic beams and flagstone floors adds to the imaginative, eclectic fare served here. It's very popular with the locals. ⓐ Kensington Place ❶ 01534 734866 ⓦ www.doransbistro.co.uk ⊙ 18.00–21.45 Mon–Sat ❶ Reservation recommended

Olive Branch ££ ❽ An eclectic menu includes homemade pastas and the finest Italian sauces. Good wine list with many Italian wines. Light, modern décor and friendly staff. ⓐ 35–39 Colomberie ❶ 01534 615993 ⊙ 12.00–14.00, 18.00–21.30 Mon–Sat

Bohemia ££–£££ ❾ The new Club Hotel's restaurant has very quickly made a reputation for itself under talented chef Shaun Rankin, and is now one of the top couple of restaurants on Jersey. The ambience is sophisticated, and the food modern, using the highest quality

ingredients. In the evenings Rankin likes to produce dishes combining meat and seafood, but the lunchtime menu is simpler – and cheaper.
ⓐ Green Street ⓣ 01534 880588 ⓦ www.bohemiajersey.com
ⓛ 12.00–14.30, 19.00–22.00 Mon–Sat

La Capannina £££ ⑩ An accomplished Italian restaurant, highly acclaimed for traditional cuisine using local produce. Good wines too. Smart and formal. ⓐ 65–67 Halkett Place ⓣ 01534 734602
ⓛ 12.00–14.00, 19.00–22.00 Mon–Sat ❶ Reservation recommended

NIGHTLIFE

Despite its size, Jersey has a wide range of entertainment. Much of it centres on St Helier, where pubs and clubs keep going until the small hours. In particular, the area surrounding the bus station is where many nightlife venues can be found. Check the *Jersey Evening Post* to see what is on. Nightlife tends to be busiest during the summer months. You can choose from a band playing in Howard Davis Park to a rock band in Chambers Pub, or visit one of St Helier's nightclubs.

If your tastes are more highbrow, see what is on at the **Jersey Opera House** (ⓣ 01534 511115 ⓦ www.jerseyoperahouse.co.uk). This beautifully restored 600-seat theatre in Gloucester Street holds performances every week of touring musicals and plays. Also check out the **Jersey Arts Centre** (ⓐ Phillips Street ⓣ 01534 700444 ⓦ www.thisisjersey.com/jac), smaller theatres hosting classical recitals, plays and art exhibitions. Film lovers head for **Cineworld** in the Waterfront Centre for the latest releases.

Outside St Helier, nightlife is rather quieter. There are many community clubs offering everything from bridge to Latin, ballroom, sequence and Egyptian dance classes. Some hotels, including the Merton Hotel, provide entertainment and are open to non-residents.

St Clement & Grouville

Once free of St Helier's suburban tentacles, the hinterland of these south-eastern parishes consists of open farmland and proper villages boasting rustic inns and churches. The seigneurial manor of **Samarès** and its impressive portfolio of visitor attractions is a major draw. So too is the coastal village of **Gorey**, and the prehistoric burial mound at **La Hougue Bie**.

When you glimpse the beach at low tide, you'll see why the dramatic sea views along this part of Jersey's coastline are so popular – its amazing rock formations are exposed. The grassy hillock of **Green Island** is a particularly scenic spot, accessible at low tide; as a bathing beach, though, it is not so good. Choose your spot carefully and watch the warning signs.

As if those deadly reefs were not enough of a deterrent to invaders of the past, a string of fortress towers guards the shore. Round the headland of **La Rocque**, a fine belt of continuous sheltered sand lines the **Royal Bay of Grouville**, fringed by oyster beds, and the **Royal Jersey Golf Club** (club members only).

Take a drive along the coastal road past **St Clement's Bay** at low tide to see a strange lunar seascape of exposed reefs and rocks. It's particularly dramatic in morning light, so bring your camera. There are free parking places at intervals. Take care if you walk along the beach – the incoming tide moves extremely fast and can be dangerous.

THINGS TO SEE & DO

La Hougue Bie

Deep in rural seclusion stands a 12 m (40 ft) mound pierced by a mysterious passage entrance. This Neolithic burial site dating back over 5,000 years now has a modern-day visitor centre.
ⓐ Route de la Hougue Bie, Grouville ⓣ 01534 853823 ⓛ 10.00–17.00 (Mar–Oct) ⓘ Admission charge

⏢ *La Hougue Bie, the Neolithic burial site*

Jersey Pottery

This family-run pottery makes an enjoyable day out. Watch ceramics being thrown, fired and painted by skilled artists or have a go at painting your own design. It also has a great restaurant, café and pub (see page 27).

ⓐ Gorey Village ❶ 01534 850850 Ⓦ www.jerseypottery.com

🕙 Showroom open 09.00–17.30 Mon–Sat, 10.00–17.30 Sun

❶ No production Sat & Sun

Samarès Manor

This Norman seigneurial manor has a magnificent herb garden, plant nursery, and a café, serving fresh local produce, using herbs from the garden. A new viewing platform was recently constructed in the herb garden. You can go on guided tours of the house and the agricultural and carriage museum.

ⓐ Inner Road, St Clement ☏ 01534 870551 🕒 09.30–17.00 Mon–Sat, closed Sun (Apr–Oct); tours of house Mon–Sat (additional charge)
❶ Admission charge

TAKING A BREAK

Jersey's south-east corner rejoices in several superb restaurants with moderate prices. It's worth working up an appetite if you're heading to this part of the island to eat.

◔ *The sheltered beach at Grouville Bay*

Pembroke £ Welcoming pub drawing visitors and locals for good-value food at lunchtime and in the evenings. ⓐ Grouville Coast Road, Grouville ① 01534 855756 ⓒ Food served 12.00–14.15, 18.00–20.15

Jersey Pottery Restaurants £–£££ After much-deserved praise in several top food guides, these three eateries, which include a gastro pub (the Castle Green), the more refined Garden Restaurant and a café (Spinnakers Bar and Grill) catering for families, are now just as prestigious as the pottery. ⓐ Gorey Village, Grouville ① 01534 850850 ⓦ www.jerseypottery.com ⓒ Opening times vary; check website or phone for details

Green Island ££ Occupies a prime location overlooking the dramatic coastline of St Clement's Bay. Modest price-tags yet very interesting cooking (the owner is a celebrated Jersey restaurateur). Terrace tables. ⓐ Green Island, St Clement ① 01534 857787 ⓒ 12.00–14.30, 19.00–21.30 Tues–Sat, Sun lunch, closed Mon

AFTER DARK

Restaurants
Borsalino Rocque ££ A large, popular place, smart but friendly, with a huge menu. Book ahead for the conservatory. Lunches are moderate; dinners pricier. Disco dancing some evenings. ⓐ La Grande Route des Sablons, Grouville ① 01534 852111 ⓒ 12.00–14.30, 18.45–21.30 Wed–Mon, closed Tues

Village Bistro ££ An innovative menu that has become known on Jersey's gastronomic scene. Local produce is used to good effect in appetising modern dishes. Set menus represent excellent value. ⓐ Gorey Village, Grouville ① 01534 853429 ⓒ 12.15–14.00,19.00–21.00 Tues–Sat, Sun lunch, closed Mon

St Martin & Trinity

Jersey's north-east parishes encompass the island's highest point, and some of its prettiest and most rural scenery. North of Gorey is a series of quiet, sandy bays – safe and unpolluted. Along the rugged northern shore, cliffs soar to a height of 120 m (400 ft) above the picturesque fishing harbours of **Rozel** and **Bouley Bay**. Inland, a web of secretive country lanes conceals dignified and prosperous-looking farmsteads.

One of these, **Les Augrès Manor**, now hosts the world-famous zoo and breeding centre set up by the author and naturalist, the late Gerald Durrell. Other popular sights in this part of Jersey are **Mont Orgueil Castle** in Gorey, and the exotic, riotously colourful blooms of the **Eric Young Orchid Foundation**. The massive breakwater at **St Catherine's Bay** provides a popular pier for amateur fishermen.

More ominous is the rocky outcrop called **Geoffrey's Leap**, where condemned criminals were forced to plunge to their deaths in medieval times. The steep slopes behind Bouley Bay are the scene of an annual motorised hill-climbing championship. And, if the distant views of the **Cotentin Peninsula** in Normandy prove tempting, you can take a day-trip to France from Gorey Harbour (you will need your passport).

THINGS TO SEE & DO

Durrell Wildlife Conservation Centre (Jersey Zoo)

The late Gerald Durrell's imaginative sanctuary and breeding centre has won many awards for its ground-breaking contribution to wildlife conservation. Rare species are rescued from the brink of extinction, and reintroduced to the wild. An informative, entertaining and inspiring place, with a friendly, direct approach to visitors and fine grounds. The Café Dodo is a good bet for lunch or afternoon tea.

ⓐ Les Augrès Manor, Trinity ⓣ 01534 860000 ⓦ www.durrellwildlife.org
ⓛ Daily 09.30–18.00 (summer); 10.00–17.00 (winter, except Christmas Day) ⓘ Admission charge

Eric Young Orchid Foundation

Plant-loving visitors beat a path through tiny lanes to these exotic hothouses where the lifetime's work of an orchid addict can be seen. High summer is not the best time to visit, but there are gorgeous flowers all year round in an astonishing range of shapes and colours. ⓐ Victoria Village, Trinity ① 01534 861963 🕒 10.00–16.00 Wed–Sat (all year) ① Admission charge

Gorey Village

The picturesque cluster of harbour cottages dwarfed by Jersey's oldest castle makes a classic photo opportunity. Besides excellent restaurants, shops, crafts and pubs, the area around Gorey boasts several first-rate sights and the village overlooks a magnificent beach. More good beaches and pretty countryside lie nearby. Needless to say, it is popular in high season.

● *A gorilla at the Durrell Wildlife Conservation Centre*

Mont Orgueil Castle

Reopened in 2006, after a £4.5 million repair programme, this splendid fortress has dominated Grouville Bay and Gorey Village since the 13th century, and is in remarkable condition, with many areas which were formerly inaccessible now open to the public. Exhibitions inside recount its history. Lovely rampart views.

ⓐ Gorey, St Martin ❶ 01534 853292 ● Daily 10.00–18.00 (Apr–Oct); 10.00–dusk Fri–Mon (winter) ❶ Admission charge

Pallot Heritage Steam Museum

Steam engines, farm machinery, theatre organs and other bygones. Occasional steam train rides and special events.

ⓐ Rue de Bechet, Trinity ❶ 01534 865307 ● 10.00–17.00 Mon–Sat, closed Sun (Apr–Oct) ❶ Admission charge

▲ The well-maintained Mont Orgueil Castle

Queen's Valley Reservoir

The quiet reservoir of Queen's Valley, inland from Gorey, is also a nature reserve. The pathways leading round its edges make a gentle 3-km (2-mile) stroll. Take a picnic with you, or combine a walk with a visit to the nearby Jersey Pottery (see page 25) and its excellent brasserie/restaurants. There are additional car parks at either end of the reservoir. 🕐 Daylight hours

TAKING A BREAK

Drive Inn BBQ £ Popular with families for its generous helpings of chargrilled meat and fish served on a flower-decked terrace or in Western-style wagons. Self-service salad bar – eat as much as you like. ⓐ Gorey Coast Road, St Martin ⓘ 01534 851266 🕐 12.00–15.00, 17.00–22.00 (summer); 17.30–22.00 (winter)

Hungry Man £ This simple snack bar, popular for decades, is the place for burgers, cream teas and the like. ⓐ Rozel Pier ⓘ 01534 863227 🕐 09.30–16.00

Royal St Martin £ Renowned for its excellent bar food, this landmark village pub in the centre of St Martin also has a separate restaurant. Good real ales. Families welcome. ⓐ Grande Route de Faldouet, St Martin ⓘ 01534 856289 🕐 12.00–14.15 daily, 18.00–20.30 Mon–Sat

Navigator ££ Perhaps the best choice in Rozel harbour – particularly if you like fish and seafood accompanied by fine views. ⓐ Granite Corner, Rozel Harbour, Trinity ⓘ 01534 861444 🕐 12.00–14.30, 18.00–22.30

Rozel Bar and Restaurant ££ A cosy pub near the bay serving good food, particularly fish. The lunchtime menu is more traditional and less expensive, and the dinner fare is excellent. Outdoor spaces include a beer garden. Pub games are also available. Children welcome. ⓐ La Vallee de Rozel, St Martin ⓘ 01534 869801 🕐 Food served

12.00–14.15, 18.30–21.15, closed Mon in winter ❶ Booking recommended in high season

AFTER DARK

Restaurants

Suma's ££ This attractive venture offers discerning palates a chance to try first-class Mediterranean cooking at affordable prices. Under the same management as Longueville Manor (see page 48), Suma's has an airy upstairs dining room, simple but stylish, overlooking Gorey Harbour. Good-value set lunches, an in-house bakery and a good wine list. Children welcome. ⓐ Gorey Hill, St Martin ❶ 01534 853291 ❶ 12.00–14.15, 18.15–21.30 (closed mid-Dec to mid-Jan)

Le Frère Restaurant ££–£££ Sitting at the top of Rozel Bay, the 'Frère' is a seafood haven, perfect for special occasion meals. ⓐ Rozel Bay, St Martin ❶ 01534 861000 ❶ Tues–Sun for lunch, Tues–Sat for evening meals ❶ Booking required

Château La Chaire £££ This luxury hotel-restaurant occupies a beautiful and secluded spot near the tip of the island. It's an elegant place, so book ahead and dress up. Cooking is ambitious 'modern British', and very fish oriented. The oak-panelled restaurant has a conservatory extension. Dining on the terrace in summer. ⓐ Rozel Bay, St Martin ❶ 01534 863354 ⓦ www.chateau-la-chaire.co.uk ❶ 12.00–14.00, 19.00–21.00

St John & St Mary

Cliff paths stretch along Jersey's scenic northern headlands, offering beautiful but taxing walks. There isn't much sand between **Bonne Nuit Bay** and **Grève de Lecq**, but energetic walkers can explore many minor natural features, such as the **Wolf's Caves** or the **Devil's Hole**. Take care with cliffs and tides and watch out for warning signs.

This rugged coastline, some of it National Trust land, is best explored on foot as the roads do not run by the sea. A blaze of wild flowers can be seen in spring and early summer and the area is a haunt of rare birds. It isn't always quiet, though – isolated headlands sometimes reverberate to the sounds of motorcycle scrambling or rifle shooting, and there are seasonal flickers of nightlife if you are out after hours at Grève de Lecq and Wolf's Caves.

● *Enjoy the wonderful views from Jersey's north coast footpaths*

There are a few small prehistoric sites, including tumuli dating from around 3500 BC. L'Île Agois was once an islet hermitage and can be reached at low tide. The hinterland is quiet and agricultural, scattered with fine examples of domestic architecture. For more information on this part of the island it is a good idea to visit the **North Coast Visitor Centre**, housed in the Napoleonic barracks at Grève de Lecq.

For a closer look at some of Jersey's traditional farmhouses visit such tourist attractions as **La Mare Wine Estate**. Another fine building, **The Elms**, is the Jersey National Trust HQ. Most imposing of all is **St John's Manor**, a classically proportioned house open occasionally for charity events.

● *See the view then taste the brew, at La Mare Wine Estate*

THINGS TO SEE & DO

La Mare Wine Estate

Jersey's only commercial vineyards were planted in 1972 in the grounds of a fine 18th-century farmhouse. It produces in the region of 30,000–40,000 bottles of wine per season, along with its renowned cider and Calvados (apple brandy). La Mare also produces preserves, traditional black butter and chocolates, which can be tasted and bought on site. There's an adventure playground for the children – and now a smart restaurant as well.

ⓐ St Mary ⓣ 01534 481178 ⓦ www.lamarevineyards.com ⓛ 10.00–17.00 Mon–Sat (Mar–Oct) ⓘ Admission charge

North Coast Visitor Centre (Grève de Lecq Barracks)

Housed in the neat, symmetrical buildings of a 19th-century Napoleonic-era barracks, this National Trust-owned visitor centre has displays and literature on history, footpaths and wildlife.

ⓐ Grève de Lecq, St Mary ⓣ 01534 483193 ⓛ 10.00–17.00 Wed–Sat, 13.00–17.00 Sun (May–Sept)

TAKING A BREAK

Teashops and good-value snacks in pubs dominate the eating scene here, but don't expect anything very elaborate. Evening restaurants are in short supply.

Les Fontaines Tavern £ Location is one of this old granite pub's selling points, as it has spectacular ocean views. Inside it has lots of character – inglenooks, ship's timber beams and an ancient cider press. Randall's ales and inexpensive bar food served at lunchtime and dinner. Children's play area. ⓐ Route du Nord, St John ⓣ 01534 862707 ⓛ Daily 11.00–23.00

St Mary's Country Inn £ One of the best examples of a Jersey speciality – the family-friendly country pub. Civilised and welcoming, it offers a

hearty range of lunchtime and evening food. There's a family conservatory room and tables outside for alfresco summer dining.
ⓐ St Mary ⓣ 01534 482897 ⓛ Daily 10.00–23.30

The Vineyard £ The restaurant attached to La Mare Wine Estate is a pleasant place for a snack, a glass of wine or cup of tea with home-made cakes. There are tables on the terrace in fine weather. You may be able to taste some home produce here, including cider or perhaps even Calvados. ⓐ Rue de la Hougue Mauger, St Mary ⓣ 01534 481178
ⓛ 10.00–17.00 Mon–Sat (Apr–Oct); 10.00–16.00 Mon–Fri (Nov–Dec)

◯ *Fruits of the sea tempt gourmets to indulge*

St Ouen

St Ouen (pronounced 'won') is Jersey's largest parish. It makes up the north-west corner of the island, a varied and beautiful stretch of striking coastline and quiet farmland. Much is still uncultivated and it is good place for walkers and nature-lovers. Coastal paths follow most of the shore, partly on breezy clifftops, partly beside peaceful dunes. There are some dangers on this exposed Atlantic seaboard, though, so watch out for warning signs.

St Ouen boasts a large number of visitor attractions, though few merit more than a 'see if passing' rating. Many are clustered around

● *The popular family beach at Grève de Lecq*

L'Etacq and **St Ouen's Bay**. If you're keen on wildlife visit the **Kempt Tower** to learn more about Jersey's flora and fauna, or perhaps take part in a guided walk through the reedbeds and lagoons behind St Ouen's Bay.

Grève de Lecq and **Plémont Bay** are two of Jersey's most appealing smaller beaches, while the giant 8-km (5-mile) strand of St Ouen's Bay attracts surfers. Inland, the manor and church of St Ouen hark back to feudal times.

It's tempting to put your foot down if you are driving on the long straight road behind St Ouen's Bay. **La Route des Mielles** is one of the few stretches on Jersey where this is possible. Be careful if you're walking across this road – especially with young children. If you are driving, remember the island's speed limit is only 65 km/h (40 mph).

THINGS TO SEE & DO

Battle of Flowers Museum

A display of floats from Jersey's colourful annual parade, which usually takes place in August. Many of the award-winning floats were handmade by museum founder Florence Bechelet. There's a taped commentary.

❸ Mont des Corvées, St Ouen ❶ 01534 482408 ● Daily 10.00–17.00 (Easter–Oct) ❶ Admission charge

Bouchet Agateware Pottery

A unique and secret process developed by founder Tony Bouchet is behind the stunning marbled clay pieces created in this tiny pottery. Visit the showroom and find out more.

❸ Rue des Marettes, St Ouen ❶ 01534 482345 ● Daily 09.00–17.00 (summer), limited opening times in winter

Jersey Pearl

Simulated and cultured pearl jewellery is on show and sale here, alongside other precious and semi-precious gems and watches. Find out what the largest pearl in the world looks like. There are workshop demonstrations and exhibitions as well as tearooms and gift shops.

ⓐ North End Five Mile Road, St Ouen (also at Jersey airport and Gorey Pier shop) ⓣ 01534 862137 ⓒ 10.00–17.30 (summer); 10.00–16.30 (winter)

Kempt Tower

The stumpy Martello tower at the north end of St Ouen's Bay houses a visitor centre (complete with video theatre) dedicated to Jersey's natural history, as well as a surfing exhibition. Nearby is the Frances Le Sueur Centre (an environmental information and education base which has been instrumental in restoring the island's floral habitat, including the protection of orchids) and Les Mielles, a nature reserve that is home to many wild flowers and butterflies.

ⓐ St Ouen's Bay ⓣ 01534 483651 ⓒ 14.00–17.00 Tues–Sun (Apr–Oct)

ⓘ Free guided nature walks on Thur in summer. Admission charge

⬥ *Windsurfing at St Ouen's Bay*

Picnic spots

The clifftop walk between Grève de Lecq and L'Etacq offers some panoramic views. Plémont Point is a good spot for birdwatching: auks, fulmars and shags build nests on the cliffs, while pipits and linnets flit across the open heathland behind. On a fine day, the 14th-century ruins of Grosnez Castle, 60 m (200 ft) above sea level, make a scenic vantage point. Further round the headland, by the water's edge, is the rock spire Le Pinacle. A sea cave is exposed at low tide and wild flowers carpet the treeless expanses of Les Landes in spring.

TAKING A BREAK

Colleen's Café £ A simple but good café, not open in the evenings.
ⓐ Grève de Lecq Pier, St Ouen ❶ 01534 481420 🕐 08.30–17.00

Moulin de Lecq £ The watermill theme of this delightful place makes it instantly appealing; see the machinery gears turning as you order drinks at the bar. Log fires, real ales and generous bar food add to the olde-worlde character. There's a children's playground and alfresco dining in the summer. ⓐ Grève de Lecq, St Ouen ❶ 01534 482818 🕐 12.00–14.15, 18.00–21.00

Plemont Beach Café £ Only open during the day, but a reliable choice for a simple meal. ⓐ La Route de Plemont ❶ 01534 482005 🕐 09.00–17.00 Wed–Sun

St Peter & St Brelade

St Peter is the first landfall for most visitors to Jersey – the island's airport is here. St Brelade, in the south-west corner, is one of the best-known and best-loved of Jersey's parishes. Meanwhile, **St Brelade's Bay** is the island's most attractive beach resort, basking amid palm-fringed gardens. It boasts of being the most southerly seaside town in the British Isles – a claim occasionally challenged by St Helier.

Though somewhat suburban in parts, both parishes have surprising swathes of unspoilt greenery. **St Peter's Valley** is one of Jersey's prettiest and greenest drives. With two separate stretches of coastline, St Peter offers access to Jersey's largest beaches and a variety of watersports facilities. It also has one of Jersey's most ambitious attractions, **The Living Legend**, which includes The Jersey Experience (a re-creation of Jersey through the ages), adventure golf, and craft shops among its many features.

⬤ *St Brelade's Bay remains largely unspoilt*

⬤ *Sun and sand at St Brelade's Bay*

St Brelade capitalises on the fact that it has one of Jersey's best family beaches. Glorious peaceful coves nestle between rocky headlands to either side, and rare wildlife haunts the open spaces behind. Beyond the fortified promontory of Noirmont, St Aubin has a distinctive salty character and is home to the prestigious Royal Channel Island Yacht Club and the nearby **Shell Garden** (see pages 102–3). Other sporting interests are well catered for – there is tenpin bowling, several golf courses and a major leisure centre. It's a good place for energetic families, with lots of clifftop walks.

THINGS TO SEE & DO

Corbière Point

One of Jersey's most glorious yet rugged spots. Head out here with your camera and watch as the lighthouse becomes silhouetted against the sunset. At low tide you can walk across to it on a rocky causeway, but check the tide tables first as the rush of water can be extremely powerful and makes the area particularly dangerous.

Fisherman's Chapel

The stippled frescoes in the early Norman chapel behind St Brelade's Bay look as though an agile leopard has had a shot at wall-painting with its paws.

ⓐ St Brelade's Bay ❶ Donations welcome

Jersey Lavender Farm

Lavender is grown and harvested on the farm, and the oil is then extracted and blended into cosmetics and toiletries. Visit the farm, the distillery and, of course, the shop. A good time to visit is between early June and late July when you can see – and smell – the stunning swathes of lavender. There is also a small café.

ⓐ Rue du Pont Marquet, St Brelade ❶ 01534 742933 ◷ 10.00–17.00 Tues–Sun (May–Sept) ⓦ www.jerseylavender.co.uk ❶ Admission charge

The Living Legend

One of Jersey's foremost attractions, The Living Legend village includes a multi-media presentation of the island's story with many special effects (known as The Jersey Experience). Housed within the same complex of landscaped grounds and play areas is adventure golf, a craft and shopping village, a restaurant, an ice-cream parlour and a fudge factory.

ⓐ La Rue du Petit Aleval, St Peter ❶ 01534 485496
◷ Daily 09.30–17.00 (Apr–Oct); Sat–Wed 10.00–17.00 (Mar and Nov)
ⓦ www.jerseyslivinglegend.co.je ❶ Admission charge

Le Moulin de Quétivel

A well-restored 18th-century watermill owned by the Jersey National Trust. See the mill wheel in action and buy stone-ground flour.

ⓐ Mont Fallu, St Peter ❶ 01534 745408
◷ 10.00–16.00 Sat (May–Sept) ❶ Admission charge (free to National Trust members)

TAKING A BREAK

Old Portelet Inn £ An excellent place for families, this converted farmhouse inn occupies a splendid location above Portelet Bay. Great-value bar food and ales and friendly service. There are outside tables and music some evenings. 🅐 Portelet, St Brelade 🅣 01534 741899 🅛 Tues–Sun for lunch and evening meals

Smugglers Inn £ Down by the beach at Ouaisné, this traditional family pub serves wholesome lunches and dinners, and is popular after a day on the beach. 🅐 Ouaisné, St Brelade 🅣 01534 741510 🅛 12.00–14.00, 18.00–21.00, closed Sun evening in winter

Old Court House Inn ££ A fine historic building right on the harbour front, as popular for the character of its interior and friendly service as for its excellent food and ales. You may remember it as the well-used backdrop to the 1980s *Bergerac* TV detective series. 🅐 St Aubin's Harbour, St Brelade 🅣 01534 746433 🅛 12.30–14.30, 19.00–22.00

The Salty Dog Bar & Bistro ££ Concentrating on fusion food, with influences from around the world, but based on local ingredients, this is a local favourite. 🅐 Le Boulevard, St Aubin, St Brelade 🅣 01534 742760 🅛 12.30–14.15 Fri–Sun, 18.00–21.30 Mon–Fri, 19.00–21.30 Sat

Ocean Restaurant ££–£££ If you want a special treat head to the smart restaurant at the swish Atlantic Hotel. On a good day, you can enjoy great views, matched by Mark Jordan's acclaimed cooking – based on the finest fresh local ingredients (they even have scallops specially caught by a diver) and presented to the highest standards. 🅐 Le Mont de la Pulente, St Brelade 🅣 01534 744101 🅛 12.30–14.30, 19.00–22.00

CORBIÈRE WALK

Since 1936 when the railway station at St Aubin was destroyed by fire, the track used by the Jersey Railway has remained undeveloped. The line opened in 1870, linking St Helier with St Aubin on the opposite side of the bay. By 1884 it had been extended west to Corbière Lighthouse, which is one of Jersey's most photographed landmarks. After the fire, Jersey Railway ceased to operate. The route today provides an easy and popular walk, about 14 km (8 miles) there and back, through interesting and varied scenery (see map page 6). The round trip takes approximately 3–4 hours, though there are good bus services operating at both ends: buses nos. 12, 12a and 15 run from St Helier to St Aubin, while bus no. 12 returns from Corbière. In hot weather, it is best to wear a sunhat and take bottled water; binoculars are useful for birdwatching.

From St Aubin's Harbour, the main road turns inland at a junction marked 'Railway Walk Corbière'. This path is the start of the track, which runs along the main road at first but gradually slips away into deep countryside. The first couple of miles after this is woodland. A little way along you cross under a road. Keep an eye out for rare wildlife such as the kingfisher and red squirrel.

Further on you approach a built-up area – Les Quennevais (pronounced 'ken'evay'). The path leads under the busy main road before rising gently as you pass the sports centre. Further on, look to your right to see the edge of La Moye Golf Course and some school playing fields. You'll get glimpses of the Blanches Banques dunes and the sweep of St Ouen's Bay, too. For the following mile or so the route criss-crosses roads and lanes, leading you back into quieter wilderness.

At the end of the route you can see Corbière Lighthouse, which is particularly photogenic at sunset after a warm day. If the tide is out you can venture across the causeway, taking care not to be stranded later by the incoming tide.

St Lawrence & St Saviour

You'll certainly find yourself travelling through these two central parishes at some stage. They suffer somewhat from their proximity to St Helier, with busy traffic routes and built-up areas, but St Lawrence has a number of interesting sights. The huge bay of **St Aubin's** is a fine, firm crescent of sand, if rather spoilt by the busy road running directly behind.

Two of the most interesting attractions in St Lawrence are the **Jersey War Tunnels**, an amazing complex of underground tunnels constructed in the last war, and the **Hamptonne Country Life Museum**, run by the Jersey Heritage Trust and occupying one of the finest farmhouses in the parish.

As you drive around, you'll see other impressive examples of Jersey's vernacular (or domestic) architecture too. Several of these are looked after by the National Trust for Jersey (though not open to the public). Look out for **Morel Farm**, and **Le Rât Cottage**.

A couple of churches are worth visiting, too: **Millbrook's Glass Church** is decorated with astonishing Lalique glasswork, while **St Saviour's Church** is the last resting place of the dashing Emilie Charlotte le Breton, better known as Lillie Langtry. Nearby is the imposing residence of the Lieutenant Governor, the Queen's representative on Jersey.

THINGS TO SEE & DO

The Glass Church

The exterior of St Matthew's Church near Coronation Park is unremarkable, but it contains wonderful artefacts in moulded white glass made by the famous French glassmaker and jeweller René Lalique. Dating from 1932, they were commissioned by the widow of the founder of Boots the chemist. The main doors are glass, as are the font and the altar cross, and there is an exquisite set of art deco angels.

ⓐ Milbrook, St Lawrence ⓣ 01534 720934 ⓛ 09.00–dusk Mon–Fri, closed Sat ❶ Donations welcome

Hamptonne Country Life Museum
A highly enjoyable folk museum comprising a reconstruction of Jersey's rural heritage over the past 300 years, craft demonstrations, a nature trail and farm animals. It was used as the location (in 2005) for the TV series of Thomas Hardy's *Under the Greenwood Tree*.
ⓐ La Rue de la Patente, St Lawrence ⓣ 01534 863955 ⓛ 10.00–17.00 (mid-Mar–Oct) ⓘ Admission charge

Jersey Goldsmiths
This widely promoted attraction is featured on many sightseeing tours. It is set in the parish of St Lawrence in Lion Park, where you can picnic in the attractive landscaped gardens or buy a light snack at the on-site restaurant. Exhibitions include designing with precious stones, the

🔺 *The Glass Church*

history of gold, and celebrity memorabilia. There is an opportunity to watch craftsmen at work, and see a huge range of costume jewellery, much of it plated in 18-carat gold. Repairs and adjustments are carried out. There's also a garden terrace restaurant.

🅐 Lion Park, St Lawrence ☎ 01534 482098 🕓 09.30–17.00

Jersey War Tunnels

This graphic and moving evocation of the Occupation period is set in a complex of tunnels dug by forced labour and equipped as a hospital for German casualties, with fascinating reconstructions and film footage. This place is a must if you're interested in World War II.

🅐 Les Charrières Malorey, St Lawrence ☎ 01534 860808 🕓 10.00–18.00 (Feb–Dec) 🛈 Admission charge

TAKING A BREAK

British Union £ Right in the centre of the island, this popular roadside pub serves simple bar food. Pleasant service. Games room and playhouse. 🅐 Main Road, St Lawrence ☎ 01534 861070 🕓 12.00–14.00, 18.00–20.30 (except closed Sun eve & Mon lunch)

The Hamptonne Café £ The Country Life Museum's attractive café will organise a picnic for you to eat in the meadow, and also serves snacks and teas throughout the day. Typical Jersey recipes on offer. 🅐 La Rue de la Patente, St Lawrence ☎ 01534 862698 🕓 10.00–17.00 (Apr–Oct)

Longueville Manor £££ One of Jersey's most celebrated restaurants in a country house hotel. Smart and formal but very comfortable, with a courteous, welcoming service. Fine gastronomy menus using homegrown fruit, vegetables and herbs. Vegetarian options.

🅐 Longueville Road, St Saviour ☎ 01534 725501
🅦 www.longuevillemanor.com 🕓 12.30–14.00, 19.00–22.00

⊙ *Looking across St Aubin's Bay towards St Aubin's harbour*

Beach tour

Jersey tilts southwards like a solar panel, which means it catches plenty of sunshine. The largest beaches lie along its eastern, western and southern sides (see map on page 6). The cliff-edged northern coast has much smaller beaches, though these include some of the prettiest on the island. This brief coastal tour leads clockwise from St Helier.

St Aubin's Bay A huge arc of gentle sand, so flat and smooth that it was used as an aircraft runway before the war. St Aubin's pretty houses and quayside bistros rise from a harbour full of smart pleasure craft. There's a large watersports complex at La Haule near St Aubin, where windsurfing, waterskiing and sailing can be organised. There's plenty of space to park.

Portelet Bay A pretty beach tucked into the steep Noirmont headland and bristling with German fortifications. Access to the beach is steep, down many steps. It has good headland walks and picnic spots.

Ouaisné Bay This sandy southerly continuation of St Brelade's Bay is much quieter than the main resort. Behind lies Ouaisné (pronounced 'Waynee') Common, an important conservation area (display boards in the car park tell you about agile frogs and creeping willow). Massive anti-tank defences constructed by the Germans act as a sea wall, but the bay is very beautiful, looking across to the wooded heights of Beauport and St Brelade. There are toilets for visitors with disabilities.

St Brelade's Bay One of the best beaches in the Channel Islands, this has a distinctly Mediterranean feel. Despite its popularity, the lovely boardwalk setting remains largely unspoilt. There are plenty of resort facilities including trampolining and various watersports. Easy access, car parking, excellent restaurants and cafés, and subtropical gardens mean you can easily spend an entire day here. Beachguards patrol during the summer.

Beauport Just beyond St Brelade's, a charming little cove ideal for a quiet picnic or walk through brambly hills. Follow the lanes from the Fisherman's Chapel. There's a steep climb from the car park.

Petit Port Another little cove near the scenic rocks of Corbière, pretty but exposed to the Atlantic. Sand and rock pools appear at low tide. There are good walks on the gorse-covered headland.

St Ouen's Bay Jersey's largest and wildest beach, dramatic in storms and not advised for weak swimmers. Best known as a surfing beach, it is also popular with joggers and sandcar-racers. Behind the bay is a low-lying belt of dunes and salt marshes, an important conservation area. It also has beach kiosks, toilets and a beachguard in summer – watch for signs.

⬤ *St Brelade's Bay*

Plémont Bay Beyond the ruins of Grosnez Castle, the beach at Plémont Bay (also called Grève-au-Lançon) appears only at low tide and has some dangerous currents, but the flat golden stretches of sand are good for games and there are rock pools and waterfall caves to explore. Beachguards patrol here in summer. Steep steps lead down from a café. Lovely headland walks are available, with rare birds and flowers on the downs of Les Landes.

Grève de Lecq A beautiful bay of golden sand, popular with families and easily reached.

Bonne Nuit Bay St John's only stretch of sand is a pretty place protected by high cliffs, and shaded towards sundown. The fishing harbour gives it character (and good crab sandwiches!). A good stretch of firm sand is revealed at low tide, but it shelves quite steeply so take care with young children. The beach café has very limited parking. There are picturesque cliff walks all around.

Bouley Bay Famed as a diving and fishing centre, these clear waters offer safe bathing in the harbour area, but are quite steeply shelving. There are steps from the café. There's a steep access road with limited parking. The harbour pier makes a popular fishing spot.

Rozel Bay This delightful wooded bay has fishing village charm and plenty of good eating places. The sparkling sea is bobbing with boats at high tide, and a sandy beach is revealed at low water. Parking here can be difficult.

Fliquet Bay Mostly rocks and pebbles, but good for quiet walks and picnics. There are no facilities.

St Catherine's Bay Sheltered by a huge breakwater, this beach has a pebbly foreshore, but some sand at low tide, as well as a café and sailing club.

Archirondel Acclaimed for its clean water, the beach here is mostly shingle, but very pretty. Beach kiosk and toilets are available, as well as parking, with wooded walks behind the beach. The small neighbouring cove of Havre de Fer has a similarly rocky setting.

Anne Port This is a shingle and sand beach just north of the village of Gorey. It is easy to reach but parking is very limited. The rocky headland of Geoffrey's Leap (south) evokes an interesting tale of a criminal who survived his death-sentence plunge to the rocks below and was acquitted, but he volunteered to have another go to show how easy it was. Second time – not so lucky.

Royal Bay of Grouville The royal appendage was added by Queen Victoria, who gave it her seal of approval. With nearly 8 km (5 miles) of sand and open common behind, it is a marvellous space for beach games and safe bathing. The exclusive Royal Jersey Golf Club lies behind, along with a string of defensive towers. The Gorey Watersports Centre provides sailing, windsurfing, canoeing, etc. It is a popular sailing bay, and there are wading birds in winter.

St Clement's Bay Jagged reefs and rock pools stretch for miles at low tide here. Choose a parking place and admire the view for a while, but if you walk down to the beach itself, beware of dangerous tidal flows.

Green Island A safer beach with good sand and in a very pretty setting. There is an excellent restaurant, with parking and toilets. You can also walk out to the 'green island' at low tide to view Neolithic remains.

Grève d'Azette Good firm sand at low tide and rocky outcrops are to be found here. There is a ribbon development behind, and there is parking at intervals.

Havre des Pas St Helier's easterly town beach, rather spoilt by traffic and buildings but with good sand and a seawater pool.

North coast drive

This leisurely car itinerary explores Jersey's north coast, heading east from St Ouen and passing through the parishes of St Mary, St John, Trinity and St Martin. You could spend a day on this route, though driving non-stop it would only take about two hours. Drive carefully – some of the narrow roads are Green Lanes and have a maximum speed limit of just 24 km/h (15 mph). It's also worth taking your binoculars for the stunning views of the other islands and France.

THE ROUTE

Start at the car park of Jersey Pearl in St Ouen, turning right out of its exit on to the B64. Soon after, turn left where the sign says 'La Saline' and then right, to head along the sea wall. Stop the car briefly to admire the sweeping view behind you of St Ouen's Bay, the largest bay in the islands. At the end of this road turn left on to the B35 and follow it up the hairpin bend. Look out for the seafood van – it's well worth stopping to check the catch of the day. Take a sharp left on to the B55. Keep an eye out for Les Landes Race Course and Grosnez Castle ruins.

Grosnez Castle

Dating from the 14th century, Grosnez is well protected by steep cliffs on three sides. The castle served as a refuge for the inhabitants when the island was raided, and some people say it is haunted. A cliff-path walk starts here and winds its way along the entire north coast, while below lies La Baie de la Vielle; this point affords the best view of Guernsey and Sark. Continue along the B55 and head for Plémont. Turn left where the sign says 'C105 to Plémont Bay' and follow this road, finally stopping in the car park at the top. If you're feeling energetic, descend the steps to visit Plémont Bay, one of Jersey's hidden gems. Afterwards, double back to the crossroads and turn left towards Leoville. Turn left again on to the B65 and follow this road down to Grève de Lecq.

◯ *Jersey's dramatic north coast, view towards Sorel*

Grève de Lecq

There are plenty of places to eat and drink at Grève de Lecq and there is a good beach, although it's not the best for swimming. The single-storey buildings on the hill behind the bay were built in the early 19th century and used by British troops as barracks. The 85-m (270-ft) mound guarding Grève de Lecq Bay has been fortified since prehistoric times and is now protected by the National Trust. From Grève de Lecq, carry along the B40 as it winds back inland. At the top of the hill you enter the Parish of St Mary – continue along the main road, passing the local school on the left. At the fork here turn left on to the C103, or La Grande Rue.

On the way look out for signs to the nearby tourist attraction of La Mare Vineyards. Still on the C103, head for Devil's Hole.

◓ *Jersey's 'Green Lanes' invite leisurely exploration*

Devil's Hole

This curious spot is not as gruesome as it may sound. Devil's Hole is the name given to a blow hole which formed as the result of sea erosion, creating a hole in the roof of a cave. A local many years ago thought that they saw an image of a devil in the cave. Take care if you choose to go down to the cave, as the climb back is a real test. Continue on the road which takes you up to the cliffs again. After about a mile you pass through one of the most unspoilt and unpopulated parts of Jersey, Mourier Valley. At the bottom turn left on to Le Mont de la Barcelone, then straight on at Rue de Sorel. You are now in the parish of St John.

Sorel

Drive down as far as Sorel Point, the northern tip of Jersey. If you look out to sea, you'll see a reef between Jersey and Sark called the Paternosters. The name originates from the sailors who used to sail past the reef reciting the Lord's Prayer as they passed, anxious to avoid coming to grief. Continue along the C100. This is a particularly good stretch for views of the other islands and rugged coastline. You can then either continue up to Wolf's Caves or turn right on to Rue de la Landes (you need good brakes for this road). Next turn left to head down to Bonne Nuit.

Bonne Nuit

Bonne Nuit Bay has many local stories attached to it. In the centre of the bay is a rock known as Le Cheval Guillaume, which used to be the site of a pagan pilgrimage; every Midsummer Day locals would take turns to row around the rock so as to avoid bad luck in the coming year. On leaving the bay turn left and head up the hill the other side (on the C98). At the top, turn left on to the B63, which becomes the C97 on entering the parish of Trinity. This is the highest point on the island.

After a while turn left on to the C96, Rue de la Petite Falaise, to head down to Bouley Bay.

Bouley Bay

There are various legends connected with Bouley Bay. Most notable is that of the Black Dog of Bouley Bay, a monstrous canine with terrifying saucer eyes that was said to roam around these lanes. The chances are that the tale was made up by local smugglers to frighten off interlopers while they brought their illicit goods ashore. The hill leading up from the bay is used for hill climb racing on occasional Bank Holidays. Head back up to the B31, Rue Es Picots, and turn left. The island's zoo is along this road, but as you really need a full day to cover the zoo properly, carry on for another half mile or so. At the next junction turn left at the C94, then left again following the sign to Rozel Bay; this road is the C93 and affords fantastic views. Head all the way down to Rozel.

Rozel Bay

Rozel Bay, often described as a wooded amphitheatre, is the smallest and prettiest bay on the north coast. After Rozel, continue up the hill on the other side of the bay, then turn left on to the road signposted Fliquet and St Catherine's Bay, the B38, which leads into the parish of St Martin. Follow this road around before turning left again on to the B91, down to the junction for St Catherine's Bay.

St Catherine's Breakwater

At the crossroads turn left and follow the road to the end, to a small car park and excellent tea room. Take your time to stroll along the breakwater to its end – the closest you can get to France without a passport! The giant breakwater at St Catherine's Bay on Jersey was one of the British Government's most embarrassing mistakes. After it was built at colossal expense in 1855 in response to threats of French attack, it was discovered no ships had a sufficiently shallow draught to use it!

A little way out from St Catherine's Breakwater you can see a cluster of three islands called the Ecrehous. During 18th-century elections, people who were known to support the minority political party were sometimes shipped out to the isles until the election was over. It is here that the tour ends.

St Peter Port, Guernsey

In a Channel Island town beauty contest, St Peter Port would win hands down. The town focuses on the reclaimed waterfront. Ferries and fishing boats chug purposefully between the bristling jetties, while the halyards of the leisure boats clank in the breeze. St Peter Port is well worth a visit and is only an hour by ferry from Jersey. From the sea, the townscape of tall granite houses rising against wooded hillsides seems enmeshed in a cat's cradle of masts and maritime rigging. Exploring the picturesque old town takes you through steep cobbled streets linked by flights of steps, with plenty of good shops along the route.

THINGS TO SEE & DO

Castle Cornet
This 13th-century waterfront fortress is a major landmark containing historical, maritime and military museums. Built in King John's reign, it was last used for defence by the Germans in World War II. At midday, red-coated retainers fire an artillery salute from the Royal Battery.
ⓐ Castle Emplacement ❶ 01481 721657 Ⓦ www.museum.guernsey.net
🕐 Daily 10.00–17.00 (Apr–Oct) ❶ Admission charge

Guernsey Museum & Art Gallery
An excellent introduction to the history of the island from Neolithic times. There's an audio-visual show and art gallery. Look out for the pretty bandstand and Victor Hugo's statue in the surrounding Victorian pleasure gardens.
ⓐ Candie Gardens ❶ 01481 726518 Ⓦ www.museum.guernsey.net
🕐 Daily 10.00–17.00 (summer); 10.00–16.00 (winter) ❶ Admission charge

Hauteville House (Victor Hugo's home)
The French writer lived as a political refugee in St Peter Port from 1855 to 1870, the period when he wrote his epic novel, *Les Misérables*.

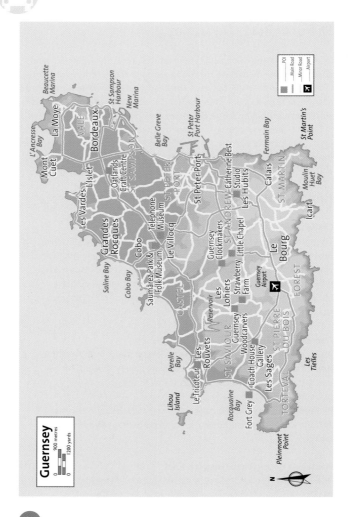

Guernsey

| POI |
| Main Road |
| Minor Road |
| ✈ Airport |

0 — 900 metres
0 — 1200 yards

Beaucette Marina
L'Ancresse Bay
La Moye
Mont Cuet
St Sampson Harbour
New Marina
VALE
Bordeaux
Les Vardes
L'Islet
Oatlands Craft Centre
ST SAMPSON
Belle Greve Bay
St Peter Port Harbour
ST PETER PORT
St Peter Port
St Catherine Best Studio
Les Hubits
ST MARTIN
Fermain Bay
St Martin's Point
Calais
Moulin Huet Bay
Icart
Telephone Museum
Grandes Rocques
Cobo
Le Villocq
ST ANDREW
Guernsey Clockmakers
Little Chapel
Le Bourg
Saline Bay
Saumarez Park & Folk Museum
Cobo Bay
CASTEL
Reservoir
Les Lohiers
Strawberry Farm
Guernsey Airport
FOREST
Perelle Bay
Les Roulvets
ST SAVIOUR
Guernsey Woodcarvers
Coach House Gallery
Les Sages
ST PIERRE DU BOIS
Lihou Island
Le Tricoteur
Rocquaine Bay
Fort Grey
TORTEVAL
Les Tielles
Pleinmont Point

N

His astonishing taste in interior décor shows a resourceful streak.
🅐 Hauteville 📞 01481 721911 🕐 12.00–16.00 Mon–Sat (Apr); 10.00–16.00
Mon–Sat (May–Sept) ❶ Guided tours only (45 min); admission charge for
house, but garden free

La Valette Underground Military Museum
Housed in a series of German wartime tunnels, this award-winning
display of Occupation memorabilia is particularly atmospheric.
🅐 La Valette 📞 01481 722300 🕐 Daily 10.00–17.00 (summer)
❶ Admission charge

❶ An excellent-value combined entrance ticket is available for four of
Guernsey's most interesting historic sights: Castle Cornet, Guernsey
Museum, Fort Grey (see page 68) and the Telephone Museum
(see page 66).

TAKING A BREAK

Duke of Normandie £ ❶ Attractively renovated 18th-century hotel-pub
with a good range of wines and bar lunches in a nostalgic maritime
setting with oak beams, fires and courtyard barbecue. 🅐 Lefevre Street
📞 01481 721431 🌐 www.dukeofnormandie.com 🕐 Daily for lunch and
evening meals

Pelican's Café £ ❷ Modern décor and friendly service in this
clean coffee shop, which serves unpretentious fare. 🅐 24 Le Pollet
📞 01481 713636 🕐 08.00–17.00 Mon–Sat, closed Sun ❶ No credit cards

The Swan £–££ ❸ This old pub serves hearty helpings of good value
traditional and more modern dishes both downstairs and in the stylish
dining room – recently refurbished – upstairs. The bar menu is available
upstairs as well as downstairs at lunch, but there is a more
sophisticated menu upstairs in the evening. 🅐 St Julian's Avenue
📞 01481 728969 🕐 All day

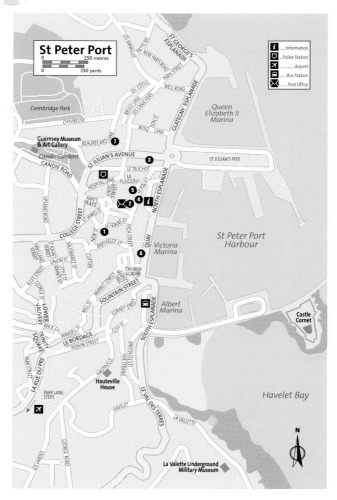

St Peter Port
0 250 metres
0 250 yards

Information
Police Station
Airport
Bus Station
Post Office

Les Amballes
New Paris Road
Pierre Rd
St George's Esplanade
Paris Street
Well Road
Les Côtils
Bruce Lane
Les Canichers
Don St
Bosq Lane
Glategny Esplanade
Queen Elizabeth II Marina
St Julian's Pier
Cambridge Park
L'Hyvreuse
Guernsey Museum & Art Gallery
Candie Gardens
Candie Road
Beauregard Lane
St Julian's Avenue
Le Truchot
La Plaiderie
Hospital Lane
Wheel Lane
Le Pollet
St Julian's Pier
Ann's Place
St James St
Upland Road
College Street
Mew St
Berthelot St
Le Febvre St
High Street
Smith Street
North Esplanade
Quay
Victoria Marina
St Peter Port Harbour
St John's St
Havilland St
Allez Street
George St
Union St
Little St
John St
Clifton
Saumarez St
New St
Market Street
Mill St
Le Bordage
Lower Vauvert
Trinity Square
Back St
Mansell St
George Road
Park Street
La Rue du Pré
Park Lane Steps
Cornet Street
Cliff St
Pedvin Street
Fountain Street
Church Square
Albert Marina
Hauteville House
The Quay
Les Échelons
South Esplanade
Hauteville
Le Val des Terres
La Vallette
Castle Cornet
Havelet Bay
Havelet
La Vallette Underground Military Museum
Les Vardes
George Road

N

Christie's ££ ❹ Stylish brasserie in the old town, overlooking the waterfront. Ideal for coffee and cakes, an early evening drink, or a full meal. Specials with Oriental and Mediterranean flavours. Live jazz most evenings. ⓐ Le Pollet ❶ 01481 726624 ❺ Brasserie 08.00–22.30, Restaurant 12.00–14.30, 17.15–22.30 (last order)

AFTER DARK

Restaurants
Da Nello ££ ❺ Intimate candlelit dining room offering classic Italian cooking and lots of seafood. Charcoal grills and pastas. ⓐ 46 Lower Pollet ❶ 01481 721552 ❺ 12.00–14.00, 18.30–22.00

Mora ££ ❻ Whether you eat a light lunch downstairs, or a fuller meal (lunch and dinner) upstairs, you will be impressed by the quality of cooking and service in this smart new restaurant, which draws its inspiration from the produce and dishes of the south-west coast of Britain, the Channel Islands themselves, and Normandy and Brittany. ⓐ The Quay ❶ 01481 715053

La Frégate £££ ❼ For a treat, book a table in this elegant hotel-restaurant at the top of the town. Panoramic views of the town and harbour and memorable French cuisine. ⓐ Les Cotils ❶ 01481 724624 ❿ www.lafregatehotel.com ❺ Daily for lunch and evening meals ❶ Smart dress required

> ### SHOPPING
> St Peter Port's waterfront stores cater for visiting yachtsmen, while shops in the cobbled streets offer a VAT-free range of classy clothes, jewellery, cameras, electrical goods, perfumes and shoes. Children will enjoy the National Trust's quaint Victorian shop (ⓐ 26 Cornet Street), or visit Guernsey Toys (ⓐ Victoria Road) for a genuine Guernsey teddy.

Northern Guernsey

The northern tip of Guernsey is easily reached from Jersey. It is low-lying and peaceful, despite being quite densely populated (in parts at least). Much land lies under greenhouse glass or water catchment systems. Here, too, is Guernsey's only significant industrial centre, **St Sampson**. The cranes and warehouses of the island's main cargo port and the power station's fuming chimneys don't often feature on Guernsey's picture postcards, but if you enjoy ambling round a working port or looking at industrial archaeology you may appreciate St Sampson's gritty authenticity. It has some useful, reasonably priced shops too.

Several Neolithic sites have been discovered in Vale, Guernsey's northernmost parish. **Les Fouillages** (small burial chambers) were unearthed on the golf course on L'Ancresse Common in 1978. Amateur archaeologists may like to track down the megalithic dolmens (passage graves) of **La Varde** and **Dehus**.

Tucked into a sheltered rock basin on the island's north-east tip is **Beaucette Marina**, full of classy-looking ocean-going yachts. If you enjoy walking or bird-watching, follow the coastal path on the headlands to see migrant birds in spring and autumn. The views are spectacular at any time of year. Castles and towers stud the headlands at every turn – **Vale Castel**, **Rousse Tower** and **Fort Doyle** are among the most impressive. Large stretches of sand and reefs lie exposed at low tide, especially in **L'Ancresse Bay** or around **Grand Havre**. **L'Ancresse Common** is a gorse-covered stretch of moor and pastureland dotted with pine trees and placid tethered cattle.

If you're an active sort, you might want to try the go-kart track just north of St Peter Port, or the windsurfing centres at **Cobo** and L'Ancresse Bays. Fishing and diving expeditions can be arranged too. All swimmers should be careful on these coasts – even the sheltered eastern side has deceptive currents.

THINGS TO SEE & DO

Guernsey Freesia Centre

For an insight into Guernsey's blooming mail-order flower business, visit these fragrant glasshouses to watch planting, picking and packing.
ⓐ Route Carré, St Sampson ☎ 01481 248185 🕐 09.00–17.00

Oatlands Craft Centre

This former brickworks houses a complex of craft studios and gift shops: glass blowing, pottery, silverwork and knitwear are just some of the things on show. Conservatory café.
ⓐ Braye Road, St Sampson ☎ 01481 241422 🕐 Daily 09.30–17.00

Saumarez Park & Folk Museum

Don't confuse this fine estate with St Martin's Sausmarez Manor, owned by a separate (and differently spelt!) branch of the ancient seigneurial family. Here, Guernsey's National Trust has set up a folk museum in the

🔺 *Saumarez Folk Museum has recreated many period interiors, like the nursery*

stable block, recreating typical period interiors, including a Victorian kitchen, parlour and wash-house. It also boasts nature trails, a children's playground, tearooms and shop.

ⓐ Saumarez Park, Castel ⓣ 01481 255384 ⓛ 10.00–17.30 (Easter–Oct) ⓦ www.nationaltrust-gsy.org.gg ⓘ Admission charge

Telephone Museum

Contains a century's-worth of long-distance communications equipment, some still in working order, displayed in a small suburban house, once a telephone exchange.

ⓐ Cobo Road, Castel ⓣ 01481 726518 ⓛ 14.00–16.30 Thur & Fri (May–Aug), 14.00–16.30 Fri only (Apr & Sept) ⓘ Admission charge. Groups can arrange visits outside these hours. Phone before to check

TAKING A BREAK

Good daytime restaurants in northern Guernsey are thin on the ground, though it isn't difficult to get a snack.

Fryer Tuck's Halfway Cafe £ More than a take-away chippie! Serves sit-down meals on the seafront, with salmon and steaks, at rock-bottom prices. ⓐ 1 Commercial Place, St Sampson ⓣ 01481 249448 ⓛ 06.30–14.15 Mon–Sat, 09.00–14.15 Sun ⓘ Licensed, with parking

Cobo Bay Hotel ££ Ambitious combinations of sweet and savoury ingredients and lots of fresh fish are on the menu in this agreeable seaside hotel. Ultra-attentive service and a good-value table d'hôte. ⓐ Cobo Bay, Castel ⓣ 01481 257102 ⓦ www.cobobayhotel.com ⓛ Daily

Hougue du Pommier ££ Non-residents welcome at this pleasant old farmhouse hotel near Cobo Bay. Filling lunch or evening bar snacks. Full à la carte menu in the restaurant. ⓐ La Route de la Hougue du Pommier, Castel ⓣ 01481 256531 ⓦ www.hotelhouguedupommier.com ⓛ Daily for lunch and evening meals

South-west Guernsey

South-west Guernsey has a strikingly varied shoreline. The west coast, scalloped into wide, low-lying bays of rock and sand, changes dramatically between high and low tide when the reefs lie exposed. With mighty Atlantic breakers, the coastline is popular with expert surfers, but novice swimmers should take care.

Round the dramatic Pleinmont headland on the south-west tip, the coast takes on a completely different character. Here the shoreline is cliff-fringed and rocky, hiding tiny, tidal scraps of sand, and the waterline can be difficult and dangerous to reach along clifftop footpaths. Defensive structures line this daunting coast, from Martello towers to German gun emplacements. Most impressive is the gaunt tower in Pleinmont. Inland lie the parishes of Torteval, St Pierre du Bois and St Saviour, which are less developed than other parts of the island. Quiet farmland is interspersed with a web of tiny rural lanes where you can get thoroughly and enjoyably lost.

Be sure to drive carefully along the west coast road in rough weather when the tide is in. The waves sometimes wash right over the sea walls – be prepared! In fine weather, though, the western seafront can be magical, especially at sunset when the rocks turn extraordinary hues of pink and gold. You can watch it from the fortified headlands, where parking places can be reached by quiet access tracks off the comparatively busy main road.

THINGS TO SEE & DO

Bruce Russell Gold & Silversmiths
Watch skilled craftsfolk hand-finishing an elegant range of jewellery and artefacts offered for sale in these 16th-century showrooms. Ancillary attractions include immaculate gardens and the Furze Oven café.
ⓐ Le Gron, St Saviour ⓣ 01481 264321 ⓦ www.bruce-russell.com
ⓛ Daily 09.00–17.00 (except Sun in winter)

Cliff walks

Guernsey's hilly south coast is the prettiest part of the island for walking. Footpaths lead all the way along, past watchtowers, coves and headlands, free of traffic but accessible by lanes with parking places at various points. Take care: the cliffs may be unstable so don't stray from the marked paths.

Coach House Gallery

Housed in sympathetically restored farm buildings, this light, airy gallery displays works by local artists, including crafts and original prints at a wide range of prices. Visit the Framecraft art shop across the courtyard for artists' materials or a speedy framing service.

ⓐ Route de Longfrie, St Pierre du Bois ❶ 01481 265339

🕙 Daily 11.00–17.00

Fort Grey

The stumpy white Martello tower on Rocquaine Bay contains a fascinating Shipwreck Museum, showing the perils of Guernsey's reef-strewn west coast.

ⓐ Rocquaine Coast Road, St Pierre du Bois ❶ 01481 265036

🕙 Daily 10.00–17.00 (Apr–Oct) ❶ Admission charge

Lihou Island

The tiny, privately owned island of Lihou, off the L'Erée headland, makes an unusual walk at low tide. There is just one house and the remains of a Benedictine priory. Check tide tables carefully before you cross; the causeway is uncovered only for a few hours.

Strawberry Farm & Guernsey Woodcarvers

Though under separate management, these attractions share facilities and can be seen on the same visit. The Strawberry Farm has turned its novel crop (over 50,000 strawberry plants in suspended growbags) into a tourist attraction, with gift and craft shops, play areas and tea gardens. The woodcarving studio produces a large range of attractive, portable

🔺 *Rocky cliffs fringe the south coast*

souvenirs and furniture from over 60 types of timber. Watch skilled craftsmen turning, carving, French polishing, furniture-restoring and cabinet-making.

🅐 Les Issues, St Saviour 📞 01481 268015 🕐 Daily 10.00–17.00

Le Tricoteur

Watch the production process then check the prices of classic hand-finished Guernseys and other woollen and cotton goods in the shop. Children's and extra-large sizes are also available.

🅐 La Rue de Catioroc, Perelle Bay 📞 01481 264040 🕐 08.30–17.00 Mon–Fri, 08.30–16.00 Sat, closed Sun

TAKING A BREAK

This part of the island has a good range of eating places, including some of Guernsey's best. Most are easy to find along the larger roads, but you'll need a good navigator for the Café du Moulin.

Longfrie Inn £ Family-oriented country inn with plenty of satisfying but inexpensive bar food and cheerful menus for kids. Garden and play area. ⓐ Rue de Longfrie, St Pierre du Bois ① 01481 263107 ① Daily for lunch and evening meals (except Mon & Sun evenings)

Café du Moulin ££ Rapidly establishing a name as one of the island's foremost restaurants, this delightful old mill is huddled in one of the island's greenest valleys and adjoining a nature reserve. Teas and bar snacks and imaginative menus. Everything freshly prepared; vegetarian choices. Book ahead. No smoking in the dining room. ⓐ Rue de Quanteraine, St Pierre du Bois ① 01481 265944 ① Daily (except Mon & Sun evening)

Fleur du Jardin ££ This charming farmhouse inn has an enviable reputation. Traditional bar food and more interesting restaurant fare with fresh fish and game. ⓐ King's Mills, Castel ① 01481 257996 ⓦ www.fleurdujardin.com ① Daily for lunch and evening meals ① Reservations recommended

Imperial Hotel ££ Three bars, a patio and garden offer a choice of places to enjoy excellent cooking near a lovely stretch of coastline with cliff walks and beaches. ⓐ Rocquaine Bay, Torteval ① 01481 264044 ⓦ www.imperialinguernsey.com ① Daily for snacks, lunch and evening meals, with huge carvery on Sun

Taste of India ££ This traditional-looking cottage, known as Sunset Cottage, on the west coast, offers an exotic Indian-inspired menu. No extra charge for enjoying the technicolour sunsets or a stroll along the strand! ⓐ L'Erée, St Pierre du Bois ① 01481 264516 ① From 12.00

South-east Guernsey

The main roads close to St Peter Port are built up and congested with a surprising amount of rush-hour commuter traffic, but brief detours down the quiet lanes of St Martin lead to the idyllic, unspoilt headlands of **Icart** and **Jerbourg**, where secluded sandy coves nestle beneath dramatic cliffs. Icart is the highest headland on Guernsey.

More sheltered than the west coast or northern beaches, these coves are ideal for swimming, though some involve a steep trek. The best way to see this part of the island is on foot by following the waymarked coastal tracks. Alternatively, take a boat trip from St Peter Port harbour on a fine day and view the south coast from the sea.

Wherever you stay, Guernsey is small enough to allow you to choose your beach by wind direction and sun position. The beaches of south-east Guernsey are a good bet when westerly or northerly winds are blowing. They tend to be sunniest in the early part of the day.

THINGS TO SEE & DO

Catherine Best Studio

One of Guernsey's most renowned jewellery designers has a studio showroom in a converted windmill. She produces original handmade pieces using precious and semi-precious materials, in a wide range of traditional and modern designs.

🅐 The Old Mill, Steam Mill Lanes, St Martin 🅣 01481 237771
🅦 www.catherinebest.com 🅛 09.00–17.30 Mon–Sat, 09.30–17.00 Sun

German Occupation Museum

An authentic display of World War II memorabilia recounting the dark days of the German Occupation of Guernsey. The day-to-day trials of the islanders are brought vividly to life in crystal sets, diaries, press cuttings and ration books. Sample some wartime parsnip coffee in the tea rooms – if you dare!

🅐 Near Forest parish church (opposite airport entrance turning)

🕾 01481 238205 🌐 www.occupied.guernsey.net 🕒 10.00–17.00 Tues–Sun (winter times vary) ❶ Admission charge

German Underground Hospital

This dank, rambling tunnel complex, dug by slave labour, is one of the most chilling reminders of the German Occupation period on any of the Channel Islands. Despite the effort expended in its construction, it was scarcely used for medical purposes, and served mainly as an ammunition dump.

ⓐ La Vassalerie Road, St Andrew 🕾 01481 239100 🕒 10.00–12.00, 14.00–16.00 (June), 10.00–12.00, 14.00–16.30 (July–Aug); restricted hours in winter ❶ Admission charge

La Gran'mère du Chimquière

This ancient Bronze Age curiosity, whose name means 'the graveyard granny', stands by the gate of St Martin's parish church. The stone-carved female figure is believed to have magical powers and, even today, flower garlands and good-luck tokens are placed on her head, especially after wedding ceremonies.

ⓐ St Martin's Church

Guernsey Clockmakers & Little Chapel

A collection of barometers and timepieces, from longcase clocks to novelty watches, many made on the premises. Nearby stands the photogenic Little Chapel, which, at only 5 m (16½ ft) long, claims to be the world's smallest church. Inspired by the grotto shrine at Lourdes, it is festooned with shells, pebbles and fragments of coloured china.

ⓐ Les Vauxbelets, St Andrew 🕾 01481 236360 🕒 08.30–17.30 Mon–Fri, 10.00–16.00 Sat ❶ Chapel accessible all year; donations welcome

Moulin Huet Pottery

A cottage workshop gallery hidden in a leafy lane leading to a pretty south-coast cove. The painter Renoir was inspired by this part of the island on a visit in 1882. Have a browse at the porcelain, stoneware,

● *La Gran'mère du Chimquière*

paintings and crafts on sale, or simply watch the pottery being made.
ⓐ Moulin Huet, St Martin ⓣ 01481 237201 ⓛ 09.00–16.00 Mon–Sat,
10.00–12.00 Sun (Easter to Christmas only)

Sausmarez Manor

This impressive stately home is occupied by one of the oldest and most
distinguished families in the Channel Islands. Entertaining guided tours
of the house highlight fine furnishings and ancestral anecdotes.
Additional attractions include exotic woodland gardens, a miniature
railway and a challenging pitch-and-putt course, ghost tours, plus a new
sculpture trail.
ⓐ Sausmarez Road, St Martin ⓣ 01481 235571
ⓦ www.sausmarez.manor.co.uk ⓛ House open Mon–Thur 10.30 & 11.30
(Easter–Oct), also 14.00 (June–Sept); other attractions open 10.00–17.00
❶ Separate admission charges

RESTAURANTS & PUBS

Many of the most appealing restaurants in this part of the island are in
beautifully located hotels. Full meals can be a bit pricey, but most places
offer less formal bar snacks or teas too.

Bella Luce ££ This long-established manor hotel in a rural setting is an
island favourite. Bar meals and afternoon teas are served in the gardens
on fine days, with traditional à la carte fare in the evenings. ⓐ Moulin
Huet, St Martin ⓣ 01481 238764 ⓦ www.bellalucehotel.guernsey.net
ⓛ Daily for lunch and evening meals

Le Chalet ££ Nestling in woodland above Fermain Bay, this alpine-style
restaurant has a sun terrace and bar for light refreshments, and a more
lavish French restaurant. ⓐ Fermain Bay, St Martin (courtesy bus from
St Peter Port except Sun) ⓣ 01481 235716 ⓦ www.lechaletguernsey.com
ⓛ Daily for lunch and evening meals (Apr–Oct)

Christophe £££ Guernsey's top-rated restaurant, where you can taste chef Christophe Vincent's superb French cooking, making the most of local ingredients. Lunch is a good deal. ⓐ Fort Road, St Peter Port ⓣ 01481 230725 ⓦ www.christophe-restaurant.co.uk ⓒ Closed Mon

⬤ Almost tropical, the beautiful Fermain Bay

Alderney

Alderney, the most northerly of the Channel Islands, lies just 14 km (8 miles) west of Normandy's Cotentin Peninsula. This 2½-km (1½-mile) wide and 5½-km (3½-mile) long island is the perfect place to unwind and offers something for almost everyone.

It does not take long to get to Alderney from Jersey, or indeed to discover the attraction of its unspoilt open landscapes, wonderful cliff walks and beautiful uncrowded beaches. Good leisure facilities and friendly pubs and restaurants add to the island's natural charms. At its heart lies the delightful town of St Anne, while Victorian fortresses stud the headlands.

Alderney was the first Channel Island to introduce duty-free goods. Alcohol and tobacco prices are worth checking wherever you see the sign. You may only buy if you are leaving the Bailiwick of Guernsey directly after your stay (e.g. for Jersey or the UK).

BEACHES

Alderney has some good stretches of sand on its northern shores, most of which are fairly easy to access. Some of the fastest tidal races in the world flow past the island. Cliffs make the southerly shore difficult to reach. The varied seabirds make Alderney's coastal walks interesting, but the many fortresses, some derelict, give it a forbidding air. **Braye Bay**, protected from westerly gales by the breakwater, is best for swimming and windsurfing. Quieter **Corblets Bay** is dominated by **Fort Corblets** and has safe bathing and good surf. **Longis Bay** – another sheltered stretch of sand on the eastern coast – is also popular.

THINGS TO SEE & DO

Alderney Breakwater

This huge, Victorian granite structure on the north-west coast of Alderney extends over half a mile into the sea. Its maintenance costs form Guernsey's contribution to the British Isles' defence budget.

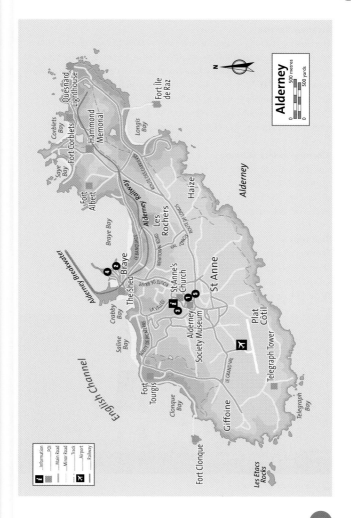

Alderney

0   500 metres
0   500 yards

Information
POI
Main Road
Minor Road
Track
Airport
Railway

English Channel

Alderney Breakwater

Fort Clonque

Les Etacs
Rocks

Giffoine

Clonque
Bay

Fort
Tourgis

Saline
Bay

Crabby
Bay

The Shed

Braye

Braye Bay

Fort
Albert

Soye
Bay

Corblets
Bay

Fort Corblets

Quénard
Lighthouse

Hammond
Memorial

Fort Île
de Raz

Longis
Bay

Alderney Railway

Les
Rochers

ROUTE DES CARRIÈRES

MOUNT HALE

LA GRANDE BLAYE

NEWTOWN ROAD

VAL DU SUD

ONGIS ROAD

Haize

Alderney

LA VALLÉE

ROUTE DE BRAYE

MOUNT DU PICOT PRÈ

St Anne's
Church

Alderney
Society Museum

St Anne

Plat
Côtil

LE GRAND VAL

Telegraph Tower

Telegraph
Bay

N

Alderney Railway

The Channel Islands' last remaining railway, built to carry granite to the breakwater, offers 30-minute nostalgia rides in old London Underground carriages during the summer. Adults and children can also enjoy a ride in summer on the miniature railway in Mannez Quarry.

ⓐ Braye Rd/Mannez Quarry ❶ 01481 822 978
ⓦ www.alderneyrailway.com 🕔 14.00–16.45 weekends and bank holidays in summer ❶ Admission charge

Alderney Society Museum

Housed in an old school, this small collection traces the island's history from prehistoric times.

ⓐ Lower High St, St Anne ❶ 01481 823222 🕔 10.00–12.00, 14.00–16.00 Mon–Fri; 10.00–12.00 Sat & Sun (Apr–Oct) ❶ Admission charge

Boat trips

Trips on *Voyager* or *Lady Maris* survey Alderney's coastal scenery – alternatively hop to France or the other Channel Islands. The Alderney Tourist Information Centre in Victoria Street has information on trips.

❶ 01481 823737 ❶ Seasonal and weather dependent

🔺 *Quesnard Lighthouse*

Les Etacs Rocks

Home to one of the British Isles' rare gannet colonies, birds sit beak to beak in a pungent top-dressing of guano. Nearby Burhou Island is home to a small group of puffins. Don't forget your binoculars.

Fort Clonque

One of Alderney's Victorian forts, attractively restored by the Landmark Trust as holiday apartments, lies at the end of a concrete causeway (inaccessible at high tide).

ⓐ Near Clonque beach

Hammond Memorial

Plaques in several languages commemorate the Russian, Polish and Jewish slave-workers who perished under German Occupation while constructing Hitler's Atlantic Wall.

Quesnard Lighthouse

Dating from 1912, the Quesnard Lighthouse offers spectacular views of the razor-sharp reefs on this dangerous coast. Afternoon visits by arrangement with the tourist office.

ⓐ Quesnard ☎ 01481 823737

🔺 *Fort Clonque, Alderney*

St Anne's Church
One of the finest Channel Island churches, built of Caen stone and restored after wartime damage.
ⓐ St Anne

The Shed
Items from a wrecked Elizabethan warship feature in this little museum.
ⓐ Braye Harbour ⓣ 01481 823222 ⓛ Some afternoons in summer

Telegraph Tower
The high cliffs near this 19th-century signalling tower offer views of all the Channel Islands.

TAKING A BREAK

Alderney offers good eating and drinking places, nearly all clustered in St Anne or Braye Bay. Prices are slightly higher than the other islands due to freight costs, but licensing hours are more lenient; pubs stay open all day and every day, including Sunday. Seafood lovers should not miss the Seafood Festival in May.

Gannets £ ❶ Attractive day-time café, licensed bistro and evening wine bar in a light, airy dining room decorated with soothing seascapes. Friendly service. Summer tables outside. ⓐ Victoria St, St Anne ⓣ 01481 823098

The Moorings £ ❷ Offers good traditional bar meals, an à la carte menu with great seafood and alfresco dining around the barbecue in summer. Good value for money. ⓐ Braye Harbour ⓣ 01481 822421

Bumps Eating House ££ ❸ Charming atmosphere with an impressive menu featuring international cuisine and an extensive wine list.
ⓐ Braye St, St Anne ⓣ 01481 823197

● *Braye Bay is ideal for swimming and offers a good choice of eateries*

First and Last ££ ❹ Primarily a seafood restaurant serving mouth-watering food that appeals to the eye and the taste buds.
ⓐ Braye Harbour ❶ 01481 823162

Georgian House ££ ❺ Civilised hotel-restaurant in an elegant period building. Specialities include seafood and traditional Sunday roasts. Good-value lunchtime bar menus, but more expensive restaurant food only in evenings. ⓐ Victoria St, St Anne ❶ 01481 822471
Ⓦ www.georgianhousealderney.com ● Daily (except Tues eve)
❶ Booking recommended

Herm

Tiny Herm (a mere 2.5 km/1½ miles long and 1 km/½ mile wide) makes a marvellous outing for a fine day. With no cars or organised attractions, the island offers a simple but captivating mix of beautiful scenery, idyllic beaches and an irresistible invitation to unwind.

You can walk round Herm in under two hours. Near the harbour is a Mediterranean-style 'village', colourwashed in ice-cream pastels and consisting of a hotel, pub and a handful of shops. Here you can have a drink, a snack or an excellent meal, and buy an imaginative range of souvenirs at good prices. Central paths take you through woods and fields past the castellated **Le Manoir**, home to 'the Tenant' (see page 86), and a tiny medieval chapel. A herd of cattle grazes in the surrounding farmland. If you strike south, you climb along cliff paths overlooking rocks and reefs, and the privately owned island of Jethou (inaccessible to visitors). The low-lying northern routes lead over heathland fringed by glorious belts of sand. Wildlife flourishes on Herm with its hosts of seabirds, butterflies and riotous flowers. Yet every artificial feature, from farm gates and fences to beach cafés and holiday cottages, is kept in tip-top order.

The early morning 'milk boat' ferry offers a reduced day return to Herm – and a longer stay on the island. Remember to listen to the weather forecast, as you'll be out of doors for much of the time.

BEACHES

Herm's pride and joy is Shell Beach, on the north-east shore. This is a magnificent stretch of sparkling quartz and shell fragments, which looks truly tropical on a fine day and is the perfect place for beachcombing, sunbathing and sandcastles. Rock pools trap fascinating pockets of sealife at low tide, and the clear, gently shelving water is ideal for snorkelling. As its name suggests, the sand consists of millions of sparkling shells, some carried from the tropics on the Gulf Stream.

Herm's northern coast is an almost continuous belt of sand and dunes at low tide, easily reached if you're prepared to walk. Near the harbour the

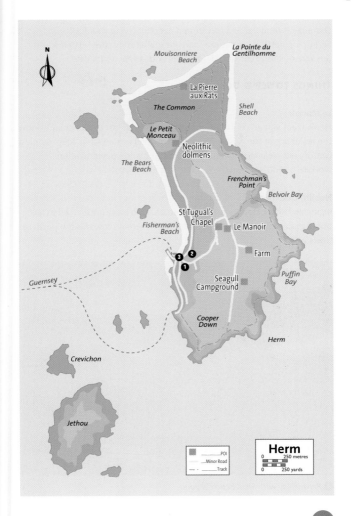

shoreline is muddier and rockier, and good for trying your luck with a shrimping net. Belvoir Bay is a more intimate sandy cove further south (beware of strong currents at low tide) with a café and toilets.

THINGS TO SEE & DO

Le Manoir

Herm's real 'village' centres around the imposing 15th-century manor, now the residence of the Heyworth family. The medieval-looking 'keep' is only a century old. Near the manor house are the island's power station, workshops and unobtrusive modern farm buildings.

Neolithic dolmens

In ancient times, Herm was considered a sacred place and served as a burial ground. Traces of several stone tombs remain towards the north of the island.

🔺 *Belvoir Bay with Shell Beach beyond*

La Pierre aux Rats

A large, prehistoric standing stone served as a seamark for centuries until quarrymen removed it in the 19th century, thinking it was just another useful lump of granite. Local sailors protested and the present obelisk was put in its place.

St Tugual's Chapel

This quaint little building dates from the 11th century. The unusual belltower is its most striking feature. It contains attractive stained glass, and a memorial to the Tenant's wife. Informal services are held every Sunday.

TAKING A BREAK

Some summer ferry tickets include lunch or dinner, but Herm operates seasonally, and in the winter the island's pubs and cafés may be closed. Check before you sail. There is a small grocery shop, or you can always take a picnic.

🔺 *Herm's beautiful Shell Beach*

The Mermaid Tavern £ ❶ The 'village inn' offers good snacks, full lunches and evening meals for most of the year. Barbecues and outside tables in summer; roaring fires in chilly weather. ☎ 01481 710170 🕑 Daily (summer); Tues, Wed, Fri & Sat (winter)

The Ship Inn ££ ❷ This pleasant pub-restaurant is part of the White House hotel (see below), offering lunchtime fare and more elaborate evening meals at the Captain's Table (inclusive ferry/dinner packages available). ⓐ Near the harbour ☎ 01481 722159 🕑 Daily (Apr–Oct)

The White House £££ ❸ Herm's only hotel is primarily for resident guests but, space permitting, day visitors may book ahead for dinner only. ⓐ Near the harbour ☎ 01481 722159 🕑 Daily (Apr–Oct) ❶ Smart dress, no smoking in the dining room

HERM'S TENANT

In 1949, Major Peter Wood and his wife Jenny took over a long lease on the island from the States of Guernsey. Their enthusiastic enterprise and hard work has resulted in today's civilised miniature paradise. Financed by farming and tourism, Herm continues to be managed by members of the Wood family (the Major died in 1998 and his wife in 1991), daughter Pennie, and her husband Adrian Heyworth. The resident population of 50 is doubled in summer by seasonal staff. Local children are educated in the tiny island school. Herm also generates its own electricity and has its own water supply and drainage systems.

NIGHTLIFE

If sea air, good food and exercise don't suggest an early night, you may find yourself practising the age-old, but much-neglected art of conversation. To encourage social interaction, television is deliberately banished at Herm's White House hotel.

Sark

Less than 10 km (6 miles) east of Guernsey lies a quaint political fossil – a last vestige of European feudalism, although the island chose to become a democracy in 2006 – with 28 elected representatives. Less than 5 sq km (2 sq miles) in area, Sark is home to about 550 permanent residents, but welcomes over a hundred times as many visitors every year. Five hours or so between ferry rides is short shrift to give this pretty place. Stay longer if you can – especially in spring, when Sark is carpeted with flowers.

Sark is a plateau of jagged rock perching on 90-m (300-ft) high cliffs, gashed by deep valleys leading to the sea. It is almost two islands, for the smaller, southerly island, called Little Sark, is only attached to its big sister by a knife-edge ridge called La Coupée. Sark's scenery and individuality attract enough daytrippers to cause bicycle jams in high season. But if you stray off the beaten tyre-tracks, you will find secret coves and crevices all to yourself.

Like its close neighbour, Herm, Sark allows no visiting motor vehicles, and access to the island is by ferry only (helicopters may land in dire emergencies). A tractor-bus service saves ferry passengers the climb up and down Harbour Hill. At the top of the hill lies the village, which is of Toytown proportions.

The island's famous Dame, Sybil Hathaway, remembered for her courage during the German Occupation, has been succeeded as Seigneur of Sark by her grandson, whose residence, La Seigneurie, is Sark's most impressive building. Although now only a titular ruler, the Seigneur still holds a few privileges first granted by Elizabeth I in 1565. He is the only Sark-dweller permitted to keep doves, for example, or an unspayed bitch. More lucratively, he is entitled to receive one-thirteenth (Le Trezième) of the value of any Sark property that changes hands.

You can get to Sark from St Helier, Jersey, in around 50 minutes by ferry.

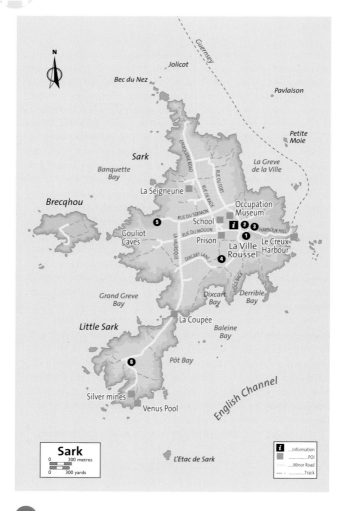

BEACHES

Access to most of Sark's cliff-backed coves involves a steep climb. Easiest to reach (from Dixcart Hotel) is Dixcart Bay – safe, sandy and scenic, spanned by an arch of natural rock. Neighbouring Derrible Bay has sand only at low tide. Adventurous explorers may discover Pot Bay or the deep tidal pool on Little Sark that is Venus Pool.

THINGS TO SEE & DO

Boat trips

If you're only on Sark for a day, a boat trip is a bit ambitious, but in calm weather it's an enjoyable way to see the island's intricate, cave-pocked cliffs and study the seabirds. Sark Tourist Information Centre (ⓐ Harbour Hill ❶ 01481 832345) has more information.

Carriage rides

See Sark the leisurely way – by horse power. Patient carthorses await the ferry boats in summer. You can pre-book a jaunt from Guernsey, or arrange ninety-minute or two-hour excursions on arrival.
❶ 01481 832135 or 07781 113386

◆ *The amazing view at La Coupée*

La Coupée

This breathtaking neck of rock, linking Little Sark to the main island, was fenced by prisoners-of-war, and is just wide enough for a tractor or a horse-drawn carriage to pass across, with dizzying drops to either side.

Le Creux Harbour

Tunnels lead to this pretty, rock-walled harbour from the more modern and practical landing stage at La Maseline.

Prison

Sark's curious little jail stands in the village. It has just two cells, and is still occasionally used before dispatching miscreants to Guernsey for trial.

Sark Occupation Museum

This museum conveys aspects of island life under the jackboot during World War II; luckily Sark escaped fairly lightly, with no serious food

● *Pretty gardens surround the manor house at La Seigneurie*

shortages and no fortifications. Items on display include photographs of the redoubtable Dame of Sark dealing with her uninvited guests.

🟠 01481 832345 🕙 11.00–13.00, 14.00–16.00 Easter–Sept

❗ Admission charge

La Seigneurie

You can't look round the Seigneur's granite manor house, but his varied, beautiful gardens are well worth seeing, with their roses, tender plants, a hedge maze and a Victorian greenhouse. Look out for the strange Gothic colombier (dovecote) and the antique cannon.

🟠 01481 832345 🕙 10.00–17.00 Mon–Fri (Easter–Oct), plus Sat & Sun in July & Aug ❗ Admission charge

Silver mines

The shafts and ventilation chimneys dating from Sark's 19th-century mining days can still be seen on Little Sark. The mines were never profitable, and were abandoned after a tragedy in 1845.

TAKING A BREAK

Sark's most sophisticated eating places are its hotel-restaurants, several of which vie for position in good food guides. If all you want is a drink or a snack, you should not have a problem; however, choice is restricted in winter, when most hotels close. Buy picnic provisions and cakes at the village's Island Stores instead for alfresco eating.

Bel Air Inn £ ❶ This inn offers a good choice of dishes with the emphasis on seafood, steaks and pasta. The restaurant has a contemporary feel. There are also two bars serving traditional cuisine.

🅐 Harbour Hill 🟠 01481 832053 🆆 www.belairsark.info 🕙 Daily

Stumbles £–££ ❷ This is one of the few places open in winter (when takeaways are also available). Have a drink in the bar, or eat in the attractive conservatory or the garden. Portions are big, and the menu

tempting – with plenty of fish and seafood options, as well as meat on offer. ➋ Rue Lucas ☎ 01481 832302 🕐 Mon–Sat (summer), Wed–Sat & Sun lunch (winter)

Aval du Creux Hotel ££ ❸ An easy place to find, with simple lunches, cream teas and dinner in a pleasant setting, as well as outside tables. ➊ Next to tourist office on Harbour Hill ☎ 01481 832036 🌐 www.avalducreux.co.uk 🕐 11.00–17.30 (Apr–Oct)

Dixcart Bay Hotel ££ ❹ One of Sark's oldest and most respected hotels (pronounced 'dee-cart') welcomes non-residents with a tasty range of snacks and full meals. Children's menu available and seafood specialities. ➋ Dixcart Valley ☎ 01481 832015 🌐 www.discartbayhotel.com 🕐 Open all year

Hotel Petit Champ ££ ❺ A west coast setting with sea views accompanies everything, whether you're enjoying sandwiches or a candlelit dinner. Serves lobster and crab. Sheltered garden. ➊ On the west coast; from the Methodist Chapel, follow hotel signs ☎ 01481 832046 🌐 www.hotelpetitchamp.co.uk 🕐 Open Easter–Oct

AN ISLAND OF YOUR OWN

'So, you like my island, Mr Bond...' A separate island, Brecqhou, lies a stone's throw off Sark's northern tip. This was privately purchased in 1993 by the wealthy Barclay brothers – twin businessmen whose reclusive entrepreneurial activities cause much local gossip. Passing ferries give a tantalizing glimpse of a huge, newly built Gothic castle rising from Brecqhou. This extraordinary lair was constructed by a Guernsey workforce sworn to secrecy. Rumours of nuclear bunkers, summit conferences and private casinos flourish, fuelled by vigorous denials, and determined resistance to trespassing.

◆ *View of the intriguing, privately owned Brecqhou island*

La Sablonnerie Hotel ££ ❶ A charming garden setting on Little Sark is just one of the attractions of this acclaimed farmhouse hotel. Others include fresh fish and home-grown produce, Sark cream teas and seafood platters. ⓐ Little Sark ❶ 01481 832061 ⓦ www.lasablonnerie.com ❶ Open Easter–Oct

NIGHTLIFE

Sark's social scene revolves round the Island Hall in the village centre, where there is table tennis, badminton and a billiard table. In summer, just occasionally, concerts and recitals are held.

SHORT TRIPS
French towns and coastline

Apart from excursions to the other Channel Islands, it's an easy hop from Jersey to France. **St Malo**, with its ramparts, cobbled streets, craft shops and fish restaurants, makes a delightful day out, and there is a daily direct ferry service operating from St Helier (journey time is 1 hour 15 minutes). If you take a car across, from St Malo, it's possible to reach the elegant seaside resort of **Dinard** on the opposite side of the river Rance (visit the amazing **Tidal Barrage** on the way). Upstream is the gorgeous medieval town of **Dinan** and, 45 minutes by car to the east, the magical abbey fortress of **Mont St Michel** rises like a mirage from the bay. Don't forget to take your passport!

❶ *The tide out in Gorey harbour*

LIFESTYLE

Food & drink

Unlike the unfortunate islanders who endured wartime occupation on grisly fare like parsnip coffee and peapod tea, today's holidaymakers in Jersey can expect good rations. Eating is an important part of Jersey life. Local ingredients, especially seafood, market garden vegetables, and dairy produce, are renowned for their freshness and quality. But many staples have to be imported, so the cost of eating out, or shopping for self-catering, may be higher than you expect.

Jersey Tourism's guides give useful restaurant suggestions, although they do not always list the more exclusive eating places. Note that since the beginning of 2007, smoking has been prohibited inside restaurants, cafés and bars.

Excellent, imaginative cooking is still on offer at moderate prices. Many tourist restaurants stay heartily traditional. Whatever the map suggests, culinary styles are closer to England than to France. Croissants and baguettes are on sale in the bakeries, but you are more likely to find a classic British fry-up on your hotel breakfast plate. Traditional carvery roasts are always popular at Sunday lunchtimes.

Dozens of friendly, family-oriented pubs offer well-tried favourites like ploughman's lunches and chilli con carne, though these are not the only things on bar menus. There is no shortage of cafés for cream teas, fish and chip shops for filling take-aways, and Indian, Chinese or Italian restaurants to provide reliable, inexpensive solutions to hunger pangs.

But there are also many good options for more refined dining, some of the restaurants as good as any in the UK. Many restaurants don't include service in the bill, so always check.

Finned or shelled, fish dishes feature on nearly every island menu. In the fast, tidal waters surrounding the Channel Islands, pollution levels are much lower than in some holiday destinations, so eating shellfish is less like playing Russian roulette with your stomach. Besides crab, brill and sea-bass, look out for Sark lobster and Herm oysters.

In the Channel Islands, humble British fish and chips attain classic status, but you will also find more elaborate French-style dishes like

● *Succulent Jersey crab for sale*

those popular in nearby Brittany and Normandy. Conger eel soup is a local favourite. Some expensive seafoods, such as spider crab and lobsters, are sold by weight rather than by portion. Check carefully when you order to avoid a nasty shock when you receive the bill.

The first glasshouses on the islands were built to grow grapes in 1795; today, huge acreages of Jersey and Guernsey are under glass, although crops have altered in line with commercial pressures. Tomatoes, ousted by subsidised imports, have often given way to flowers. Market gardening is still important, however. Jersey Royal new potatoes, boiled and buttered with herbs, are a dish fit for a queen or king. Strawberries, celery, courgettes and many salad crops are raised for local consumption as well as the export trade. You'll often see produce on sale in little hatches by the roadsides, with an honesty box for the money.

● *Jersey Royal potatoes are extra delicious here where they are grown*

Most people know about Channel Island 'gold top' milk with its high butterfat content. Butter and cream are produced in huge quantities, enriching local menus everywhere. Apart from a little Guernsey cheddar, you won't see much island-produced cheese – the milk sours too quickly.

All kinds of cakes and scones appear in tea and coffee shops. Local choices include Jersey Wonders (a kind of doughnut), fiottes (balls of sweet pastry) or Guernsey gâche (pronounced 'gosh') – a fruit tea bread. You can sometimes buy this ready buttered by the slice – good for a picnic! Don't forget to try some Channel Island fudge – available in an amazing range of flavours.

One recipe widely promoted as an island classic is known as a bean crock, or bean jar – a rib-sticking casserole of pork, beans and onions. You may also come across black butter, which, despite its name, contains no dairy products at all. It's a long-brewed mixture of apples, sugar, lemons and cider, flavoured with liquorice. Try it spread on a slice of gâche.

The Normans introduced cider to the islands, but today beer is more popular. The Channel Islands also produce their own version of a cream liqueur, rather like Baileys. You may find an apple brandy on Jersey, made at La Mare Wine Estate, as well as the estate's wine, and that of other producers. Local beers you'll see everywhere include Mary Ann (Jersey) and Guernsey Brewery ales. Randalls no longer brews its own beer, but imports real ale and owns many Channel Island pubs.

THE ORMER

The mysterious ormer (more widely known as abalone), a large mollusc like an asymmetrical limpet, derives its name from the French 'oreille de mer' (sea ear) – the Channel Islands being the northern limit of its habitat.

Unfortunately this local delicacy is now rare due to over-fishing. As such, strict regulations apply to the collection of ormers. They must only be harvested between the months of September and April, and only on the first day of the full moon and for the three days after. During this period, Jersey men and women scour the rocks to find the sought-after ormer. These rules are strictly policed and heavy fines are levied on offenders.

Once found, the ormer is prised from the underside of rocks by hand and carried to shore in a traditional ormer basket. It is then beaten, cooked in the oven as a casserole or served with gravy, carrots and onions. The ormer's striking mother-of-pearl inner shell is also used as decoration on houses and in jewellery.

Shopping

The Channel Islands market themselves as an inexpensive destination because duties are low and there is no VAT. Freight costs can erode this advantage and you should take advice before arranging for purchases to be shipped directly to the UK – you may end up having to pay VAT when they pass through customs. Also, do not forget that non-EU customs restrictions apply to any luxury purchased in the Channel Islands that you take back to the UK. Alcohol and tobacco are cheap, but savings on other goods are not always as great as you might expect.

Look out for the 'Genuine Jersey' logo, indicating that the product is, as its name implies, genuinely made or produced on the island. This means that visitors, as well as residents, can ensure they are buying real, local products. Dairy produce, honey, pottery, oysters, wines, beers, locally made jewellery, needlework, wooden artefacts and artworks are among the products that currently display this distinctive red logo.

● *Browsing for antiques in the market in St Helier*

St Helier has the best shopping centres and streets in Jersey. Start your shopping spree in the area around King Street and Queen Street. The Quennevais Shopping Centre in St Brelade is also worth a visit. The markets and some shops are closed on Thursday afternoons, although many stay open into the evening in the height of the summer. There is no general Sunday trading in Jersey.

Island crafts

For one-stop centres where you can do all your souvenir buying in one go, head for the Craft and Shopping Village attached to Jersey's Living Legend attraction (see page 43) or, when you're visiting Guernsey, head for the Oatlands Craft Centre in St Sampson.

Jewellery

Some of Jersey's largest jewellery showrooms are Jersey Goldsmiths at Lion Park, St Lawrence, and Jersey Pearl in North End Five Mile Road, St Ouen. Catherine Best, well known on Guernsey (see page 71), recently opened a shop in St Peter. Note that Channel Island gold and silver is not subject to the same rigorous assay and hallmarking process as it is in the UK. Any 'guarantee' offered with jewellery generally refers to the quality of workmanship, rather than any intrinsic value.

Knitwear

A genuine Channel Island sweater makes an excellent souvenir purchase. A classic Guernsey sweater is instantly recognisable. The oiled wool is specially stitched, twisted and seamed to repel water. Traditional, hand-finished Guernseys are produced at the Jersey Woollen Mills at St Ouen. For a sweater with a difference, try an Alderney, sold at Alderney's Channel Jumper shop near Braye Harbour on the island.

Perfume & cosmetics

St Helier is full of perfumeries, offering expensive, big-name brands, with everything from Estée Lauder to Chanel. There are a few smaller, chemist-style outlets that offer less expensive options as well.

Children

Jersey welcomes kids and there's plenty for them to do, although remember that the island has a leisurely way of life. Rushing about is not in the usual vocabulary, so be aware that children won't necessarily find lively attractions, such as theme parks, throughout the whole of the island. They will find plenty of sporting activities though, such as swimming, go-karting, horse riding and tennis, and fun holiday pursuits like beachcombing.

TOP ACTIVITIES

The high-tech **Living Legend** complex (see page 43) is one of Jersey's best all-round family attractions – an entertaining way to absorb a bit of island history.

The best museums for children are those run by the Jersey Heritage Trust, including: **Elizabeth Castle**, which offers battlement climbs and a ride on an amphibious 'duck truck' (see page 18); **Mont Orgueil**, Gorey's medieval castle (see page 30); St Helier's excellent **Maritime Museum**, with lots of hands-on seafaring (see pages 20–21); and the **Hamptonne Country Life Museum**, with its costumed interpreters and farm animals (see page 47). There's also plenty to see at the **Jersey Museum** (see page 20) and **La Hougue Bie** (see page 24). Catch a ride in the vintage **Museum Services Heritage Bus** if you're visiting the out-of-town sights.

On a wet day, the **Fort Regent** complex offers stacks of ideas to burn off energy (see pages 18–20). See what over three million pearl shells

> ### DURRELL WILDLIFE CONSERVATION TRUST (JERSEY ZOO)
> Entertaining and educational, Jersey Zoo's friendly style ensures few children escape without learning more about a range of creatures from a gorilla to a flat-tailed tortoise. There is an audiovisual show and lots of special displays on endangered species, breeding programmes or releases into the wild (see page 28).

look like at the **Shell Garden** in St Aubin. Mollusc shells have been embedded in cement to create shell churches, mermaids, boats and more. ☎ 01534 743561

aMaizin! Maze and Adventure Park is an attraction that should appeal to younger children. Apart from the maze itself (made of maize), the adventure park has plenty of activities on offer, and there is also a craft centre to keep them occupied. ⓐ La Hougue Farm, St Peter ☎ 01534 482116 🕐 Daily 10.00–18.00 May–mid-Sept ❶ Admission charge

Beachcombing
Remember those childhood seaside holidays full of rock pools and sandcastles? Jersey's beaches are the perfect place to relive those simple, old-fashioned pleasures. Armed with buckets, spades and shrimping nets, children can have days of cost-free fun. Tidal seawater pools also offer sheltered bathing for older children.

🔵 *Elizabeth Castle, the atmospheric causeway fortress in St Aubin's Bay*

Festivals & events

Jersey is host to many festivals, carnivals and special events throughout the year. Some of the biggest annual events on the island are listed below, though you'll find many other things going on. Precise dates vary from year to year, so check with the tourist office. Most are geared to the main holiday season (Easter to October). Besides the normal public holidays observed in the UK, the Channel Islands commemorate Liberation Day (9 May – the end of German Occupation) and Remembrance Sunday (mid-November) with fervour.

The colourful parade of the **Battle of Flowers**, with flower-dressed floats, is irresistible if you're on Jersey in mid-August, while St Aubin has a **food fair** in July and there's an **international air display** in September. In July, the island goes 'Wet & Wild' with a week-long **Water Festival**, including wakeboarding, sailing, surfing and scuba-diving opportunities. Other festivities on Jersey include:

- **Gorey Fête de la Mer** (May) Alfresco dining along Gorey Pier (also a fête in August)
- **Foire de Jersey** (May) A traditional country fair
- **Maritime Festival** (July) Around St Helier harbour
- **Jersey Street Theatre Festival** (July) In the streets of St Helier
- **Jersey Regatta** (September) The island's main sailing event
- **Jersey Music Festival** (September) A week of music from around the globe
- **Tennerfest** (October) A celebration of Jersey's food, with over 100 restaurants taking part.
- **Jersey Rally** (October) A motoring challenge in Jersey's lanes
- **La Fête de Noué** (December) Christmas festival

OTHER ISLAND EVENTS

Guernsey has its share of festivals and carnivals, and on Alderney there's a seafood festival in May. The island also hosts its **Alderney Week** in August with fancy dress parades, children's races and tug-of-war contests, with bonfires and fireworks to follow.

The colourful Battle of Flowers procession

Sports & activities

Jersey offers a wide range of organised sports facilities. Jersey's Fort Regent (see pages 18–20) in St Helier is a large complex that provides one-stop fitness in the form of swimming pools, tennis and squash courts. The island also has the indoor Les Quennevais Sports Centre in St Brelade, and an outdoor sports complex at the Jersey Recreation Grounds in St Clement.

BOWLS

Lawn bowls can be played in several locations on Jersey, including the Jersey Recreation Grounds. Some places have a strict dress code. If you are nipping over to Guernsey you can play outdoor bowls at Beau Séjour, indoors at Hougue du Pommier and Fort Regent. Ten-pin bowling is available at the well-equipped Jersey Bowl complex near the airport.

FISHING

Channel Island waters attract a wide range of species. Sea and wreck-fishing boats can be chartered on most of the islands.

GOLF

The enthusiasm for harrying small white balls into tiny holes knows no bounds on the Channel Islands. Egged on by resident golfing millionaires, Jersey now has half a dozen greens, not counting numerous pitch-and-putts and mini-golf courses. Two of these, the Royal Jersey at Grouville and La Moye near St Ouen's Bay, are prestigious clubs that accept only handicapped players from other recognised clubs. Less socially daunting courses are available at Les Ormes, Wheatlands, Les Mielles and Jersey Recreation Grounds. Book ahead (weekdays are cheaper) and check about equipment hire.

HORSE RIDING

Many schools offer tuition and escorted hacking. Jersey has over half a dozen stables, and a spectacularly set race course at Les Landes, where

British and French horses compete. Tourist offices can supply lists of riding schools and racing fixtures.

MOTOR SPORTS

Sand-racing, hill climbing, rallies and motocross events are organised at various times throughout the year on Jersey. The Tourist Information Office in Liberation Square, St Helier, is the best place to find out what's happening. ☎ 01543 500888

RACQUET SPORTS

Tennis, squash and badminton courts can be hired at the main sports complexes.

🔺 *Riding the surf, St Brelade's Bay*

SAILING

The ritzy marinas around the Channel Islands soon tell you these
waters represent nirvana for many yachtsfolk. If you're not lucky enough
to own some ocean-going gin palace, you can always hire one, skippered
or bareboat. Jersey is a good choice for novice sailors, although you can
sail the waters around the other islands too.

WATERSPORTS

With all that sea on the doorstep, it's hardly surprising that there's
plenty for waterbabies to do. Windsurfing enthusiasts should head
for St Brelade's Bay or Grouville Bay for tuition or equipment.
Waterskiing is available at the Jersey Seasports Centre in St Aubin.
Diving is an attractive proposition in the clear waters around the
Channel Islands, but you should take advice about currents. Wreck diving
is a speciality, and there are diving centres in St Helier and Bouley Bay
(trial dives are offered).

For novices, surfing here should probably remain a spectator sport,
but experienced surfers may like to pit their skill against the Atlantic
breakers of Jersey's St Ouen's Bay. Other watery activities include
canoeing, rowing, pedalos, jet-skiing, parascending, speedboating and
'banana boats' – available from the main watersports centres at
St Aubin, Gorey or St Brelade.

Pure Adventure caters for people of all ages and abilities who have a yen
for a seriously active time, and is able to organise Blo-Karting, abseiling,
power boating, rock climbing and many other activities. ❶ 01534 769165
Ⓦ www. purejersey.com
Jersey Kayak Adventures offers sea kayak trips around the coast.
All equipment (including wetsuits) is provided. ❶ 01534 853138
Ⓦ www.jerseykayakadventures.co.uk

---

❿ *One of Jersey's distinctive phone boxes*

Accommodation

There is a range of accommodation on Jersey, from self-catering to luxury hotels, with many now in the 4–5 star range. Book early for the high season or during special events. The tourist office website (ⓦ www.jersey.com) has links to hotel sites. The hotels below are graded by approximate price: £ = budget ££ = mid-range £££ = expensive

Westhill Country Hotel £ Family owned, with two pools and large gardens, on the outskirts of St Helier. ⓐ Monte à L'Abbe St Helier ⓣ 01534 723260 ⓦ www.westhillhoteljersey.com

Beausite £–££ Housed mainly in an old farm building, this is a good choice for families, close to the main attractions of the south-east coast of Jersey. It has a pool, sauna, a bar, a restaurant and a fine garden. ⓐ Grouville Bay, Grouville ⓣ 01534 857577 ⓦ www. southernhotels.com

The Hampshire £–££ Not far from the centre of St Helier. The best rooms have recently been refurbished to high standards. Heated pool and car park. ⓐ 53 Val Plaisant, St Helier ⓣ 01534 724115 ⓦ www.hampshirehotel.co.uk

Old Court House Inn £–££ Comfortable rooms in this old inn on the seafront, parts of which date from the 15th century. A good place to eat, too. ⓐ St Aubin's Harbour, St Brelade ⓣ 01534 746433 ⓦ www.oldcourthousejersey.com

Samarès Coast Hotel £–££ Has an outdoor pool, a restaurant, a garden and small gym and leisure centre. Some rooms have sea views. ⓐ Coast Road, St Clement ⓣ 01534 873006 ⓦ www.morvanhotels.com

Uplands Hotel £–££ Based around old farm buildings a mile from the centre of St Helier, this hotel has a pool and grounds. ⓐ St John's Road, St Helier ⓣ 01534 873006 ⓦ www.morvanhotels.com

Windmills Hotel £–££ Family run, in an excellent position with views over St Brelade and Ouisne Bays. Terraced gardens, an outdoor pool, a restaurant and parking. ⓐ Mont Gras d'Eau, St Brelade ⓣ 01534 744201 ⓦ www.windmillshotel.com

Merton ££ This large hotel is one of the best choices for families, with high-quality leisure facilities, gardens, supervised children's activities, a laundrette, and entertainment in high season. ⓐ Belvedere Hill, St Saviour ⓣ 01534 724231 ⓦ www.mertonhotel.com

Somerville ££–£££ Good views over St Aubin's harbour (a short walk downhill), well-appointed rooms and an outdoor pool. The restaurant (Tides) is one of the best locally, serving good breakfasts. The bar and terrace are also inviting. The most comfortable choice in St Aubin. ⓐ Mont du Boulevard, St Aubin ⓣ 01534 741226 ⓦ www.dolanhotels.com

The Atlantic £££ Without doubt one of the best hotels on Jersey, with luxurious rooms, an outdoor pool, attractive gardens, a small gym, parking and superb views of St Ouen's Bay. A member of Small Luxury Hotels of the World. The Ocean restaurant is one of the best in the British Isles. ⓐ Le Mont de la Pulente, St Brelade ⓣ 01534 744101 or 00 800 525 48000 (freephone) ⓦ www.slh.com/atlantic

The Club Hotel & Spa £££ A new boutique hotel in the centre of St Helier, with very high-quality bedrooms, modern décor and notable spa. It also has an outdoor pool and two restaurants, including the top-rated Bohemia. A good choice for either business or pleasure. ⓐ Green Street, St Helier ⓣ 01534 876500 ⓦ www.theclubjersey.com

Longueville Manor £££ A member of Relais & Chateaux, with a fine restaurant, luxurious bedrooms, a tennis court, an outdoor swimming pool and parking – all set in substantial grounds. The manor dates from the 14th century. ⓐ Longueville Road, St Saviour ⓣ 01534 725501 ⓦ www.longuevillemanor.com or www.relaischateaux.com

Preparing to go

GETTING THERE

By far the best way to visit Jersey is as part of an inclusive package, although travelling independently by booking a flight and accommodation is popular too. Jersey is well served by airlines, and there are both regular scheduled and charter flights from around 30 airports in the UK, including Aberdeen, Birmingham, Bristol, the London airports, Manchester, Leeds, Liverpool, Norwich and Southampton. Flights take around an hour from most parts of the UK. Travelling by sea to Jersey is easy from Poole, Portsmouth and Weymouth. For information on tour operators featuring Jersey, visit www.abta.com.

Many people are aware that air travel emits CO_2, which contributes to climate change. You may be interested in the possibility of lessening the environmental impact of your flight through the charity Climate Care, which offsets your CO_2 by funding environmental projects around the world. Visit ⓦ www.climatecare.org

Airlines include:
Bmi ❶ 0870 6070 555 ⓦ www.flybmi.com
British Airways ❶ 0780 850 9850 ⓦ www.ba.com
Flybe ❶ 0871 522 6100 ⓦ www.flybe.com

Ferry operator:
Condor Ferries ❶ 0870 243 5140 ⓦ www.condorferries.com

BEFORE YOU LEAVE

Holidays should be about fun and relaxation, so avoid last-minute panics and stress by making your preparations well in advance. You do not need inoculations to travel to Jersey, but it is worth checking that you and your family are up-to-date with the basics, such as tetanus. If you take prescription medicines, make sure you have enough to last the whole trip. Consider packing a small first-aid kit containing plasters, antiseptic cream, travel sickness pills, insect repellent and/or bite-relief cream, upset stomach remedies and painkillers. Take plenty of sunscreen as Jersey can get very hot in the summer. Don't be deceived by a cool breeze and, for children in particular, choose a high factor lotion.

DOCUMENTS

The most important documents you will need are your tickets and passport, plus your driving licence if you are planning to take your car or hire one while on Jersey. If you plan to have more than one driver of the vehicle, make sure that they, too, have their driving licence. Passports are not needed by UK citizens for travel to the Channel Islands, however you will want them if you are thinking of an excursion to France. Remember photo ID will be required by your airline (check with your airline as to what type of photo ID is acceptable) and if you need medical assistance. Make sure that your passports are up-to-date and have at least three months left to run (to be safe, six months is even better). All children, including newborn babies, need their own passport now. It generally takes at least three weeks to process a passport renewal. This can be longer in the run-up to the summer months. Contact the Passport Agency for the latest information on how to renew your passport and the processing times involved. ❶ 0870 521 0410 ⓦ www.ukpa.gov.uk. Always check the details on your travel tickets well before your departure, ensuring that the timings and dates are correct.

MONEY

Although Jersey has its own notes and coins, UK currency is legal tender in the Channel Islands so you do not need to worry about currency exchange or traveller's cheques. However, you should make sure that your credit, charge and debit cards are up to date – you do not want them to expire mid-holiday – and that your credit limit is sufficient to allow you to make those holiday purchases. Do not draw out too much money from cashpoints, as Channel Islands currency will not be accepted back in the UK.

INSURANCE

Have you got adequate cover for your holiday? Check that your policy covers you properly for loss of possessions and valuables, for activities you might want to try – such as scuba diving, horse riding or watersports – and for emergency medical and dental treatment, including flights home if required. You do not need a EHIC medical card (which replaced the E111) but you do need proof of UK citizenship to obtain treatment. For further information, call EHIC enquiries line (ℹ 0845 605 0707) or visit the Department of Health website (ⓦ www.dh.gov.uk).

CLIMATE

As one of the most southerly of the Channel Islands, Jersey has one of the best sunshine records in the British Isles. It enjoys long, hot summer days with around 2,000 hours of sunshine a year, and mild winters. Despite a deceptive sea breeze, the air is clear and the ultra-violet rays are strong. Don't forget to slap on the sun-cream.

BAGGAGE ALLOWANCE & PACKING TIPS

Baggage allowances vary according to the airline, destination and the class of travel, but 20 kg (44 lb) per person is the norm for luggage that is carried in the hold (it usually tells you what the weight limit is on your ticket); in addition you are allowed one item of cabin baggage weighing no more than 5 kg (11 lb), and measuring 46 x 30 x 23 cm (18 x 12 x 9 in). You can carry your duty-free purchases, umbrella, handbag, coat, camera, etc as hand baggage. Large items – surfboards, golf clubs, collapsible wheelchairs and pushchairs – are usually charged as extras and it is a good idea to let the airline know in advance that you want to bring these. Note that, at the time of writing, there are restrictions on the type and quantity of liquids that can be carried in hand luggage, as well as on sharp objects, for instance. But check with your airline before you fly to find out the latest information.

For your trip to Jersey, you should consider packing the following:

- Photo ID and/or passport – the latter is necessary if you think you may be tempted by the idea of hopping over to France for the day.

- Checklist of UK prices for items you may want to buy while you are on holiday. Because of low taxation and the absence of VAT, cameras, electronic goods, clothing, perfumes, cigarettes, alcohol and jewellery are all cheaper than in other parts of Europe – but not always: some retailers mark their prices up to take account of the cost of freighting the goods to the Channel Islands. Do your homework beforehand.
- Camera.
- Driving licence – you will need this to hire a car (even if you've prebooked one) or a moped. Photocopies of your licence are not accepted on the islands.
- Sensible footwear – you're bound to want to do some walking at some point, if only round St Helier's shops.
- Warm sweater – but save space in your suitcase to take home a real Channel Island jersey or Guernsey.
- Pocket binoculars and perhaps a field guide to birds or wild flowers, if you are a keen nature buff.
- National Trust card if you have one – both Jersey and Guernsey have affiliated NT branches which allow UK members free access to their properties.
- For local holiday reading, you may be interested in Jenny Wood's account of life on Herm as the Tenant's wife, or the enthusiastic books about Jersey written by John Nettles on the making of the 1980s *Bergerac* TV series. Classics include Compton Mackenzie's novel *Fairy Gold*, based on Jethou, and Victor Hugo's *Toilers of the Sea*, set in Guernsey. If you want to know more about the Channel Islands during the Occupation, Madeleine Bunting's *The Model Occupation* is a highly readable account.

CHECK-IN & CUSTOMS

First-time travellers can often find airport security intimidating, but it is all very easy, really. If you are travelling from a large airport, check which terminal before you leave home.

- Check-in desks usually open two hours before the flight is due to depart. Arrive early for the best choice of seats. Note that check-in times are normally shorter for domestic flights (including Jersey) than for international ones; and shorter from Jersey to the British mainland than vice-versa. But always check.
- Look for your flight number on the TV monitors in the check-in area, and find the relevant check-in desk. Your tickets will be checked and your luggage labelled. Take your boarding card and go to the departure gate, where your boarding pass will be checked. There are no passport controls for flights to the Channel Islands, but you will go through a security check, during which your hand luggage will be X-rayed.
- In the departure area, you can shop and relax, but watch the monitors that tell you when your flight is ready to board – usually about 30 minutes before take-off. Go to the departure gate shown on the monitor and follow the instructions given to you by airline staff.

CUSTOMS ALLOWANCES

The Channel Islands are not full members of the European Union, and allowances are less generous than between other member states. At the time of writing, you may take only 200 cigarettes, a litre of spirits, 60 ml perfume or £145-worth of other goods, including gifts and souvenirs, either into the Channel Islands or back to the UK. Check with your travel agent or tour operator for up-to-date information.

During your stay

AIRPORT

Jersey's airport is in the parish of St Peter, to the west of the island, and although it can be a longish walk to baggage reclaim on arrival, it is much quicker to get to departure gates. The departure terminal, particularly airside, has more in terms of bars, shops etc than the arrival terminal. Hire cars, buses, taxis and private transfers (booked in advance) are all available at the airport. See ⓦ www.jersey.com for more details, including a plan of the airport.

BEACHES

Jersey is surrounded by some of the swiftest currents and highest tides in the world. West coast beaches are exposed to powerful Atlantic breakers – wonderful for experienced surfers, but unsuitable for weak swimmers. Never try to cross a causeway or explore sea caves without checking the tide tables and pay attention to warning signs. Do not swim if red flags are flying (see Beach Safety information below). Lifeguards are stationed on some of the more popular beaches in summer. Other beaches may be safe for swimming but not have lifeguards or life-saving amenities available.

CHILDREN'S ACTIVITIES

Most Jersey residents will welcome children and there is plenty for them to do. There are attractions and sporting activities aimed at children, and

> **BEACH SAFETY**
> A flag system is used to warn bathers when sea conditions are unsafe for swimming.
> **Red flag** = dangerous conditions, no swimming
> **Yellow** = good swimmers only, apply caution
> **Green** = safe bathing conditions

● *Some beaches have strong currents*

the many fortifications scattered all over Jersey make tempting places for children to play and hide. Do remember, however, that some castles and ruins are derelict and may be dangerous to explore.

COMMUNICATIONS

Jersey's telephone system is as it is in the UK, though phone boxes, of which there are many, are yellow. Dialling codes abroad are as they are in the UK. Note that your normal mobile network may not be available on the island, so be prepared for higher call charges. When phoning a Jersey number, there is no need to use the 01534 prefix (except when calling from a mobile). There is widespread internet access (most hotels have it), as well as Wi-Fi coverage.

CURRENCY

Sterling is acceptable in Jersey, as it is on all the Channel Islands, so you don't need to change any money. Jersey issues its own coins and banknotes, but these are not legal tender in the UK. Traveller's cheques, UK cheques backed by a banker's card and major credit cards are all widely accepted methods of payment. There are no cash dispensers on the smaller islands.

ELECTRICITY

Jersey has the same voltage as the UK, 240 volts AC, and uses UK-style three-pin sockets.

TOURIST INFORMATION

Jersey's main Tourist Information Office is in the States of Jersey Tourism Office. ⓐ Liberation Square, St Helier ⓣ 01534 448800 ⓦ www.jersey.com ⓛ 09.00–17.00 Mon–Fri, 09.00–13.00 Sat (Oct–Mar); 08.30–17.30 Mon–Fri, 08.30–13.00 Sat & Sun (Apr–Sept)

The tourist office publishes several very useful guides as well as the informative *Pure Jersey* magazine. Another useful website for some of the main sights is ⓦ www.jerseyheritagetrust.org

> **EMERGENCIES**
> Dial 999 for police, fire, ambulance or coastal rescue services.

GETTING AROUND

Car hire & driving A hired car is the most popular way by which to explore Jersey, and rental rates are very reasonable. Traffic congestion is a serious problem on Jersey, which has many narrow lanes and blind bends, often lined with unforgiving granite walls or ditches, and no footpaths. Great care is needed on the roads at all times. Choose the smallest car you can tolerate, because the lanes are too narrow for large vehicles. Hired cars are marked with a large letter H, but locals are surprisingly tolerant of bewildered tourists blundering round their lanes. Remember that you must have a valid driving licence with no endorsements for dangerous or drunk driving in the last five years. You must be aged 21 years and over. You will need a good map to deal with the lanes. Your hire car company, your hotel or the tourist office will be able to provide one. Otherwise, you can hire satnav equipment for your hire car at the airport for a reasonable charge.

Ferries Travel between Jersey and mainline UK, France and the islands of Guernsey, Alderney, Sark and Herm is easy from St Helier. Try Condor Ferries (**☎** 0870 243 5140 **ⓦ** www.condorferries.com).

Parking Parking regulations are very strictly enforced, even with visitors. In St Helier and one or two other popular places, parking is by a paycard system. Paycards are available from shops, post offices and garages displaying the symbol, or from Jersey Tourism. You are required to scratch off the appropriate time and date as instructed and leave it visible in your car. Other areas use parking discs, obtainable from St Helier Town Hall. A paycard or disc is not required from 17.00 to 08.00 or on a Sunday. There is free parking for disabled badge holders.

Petrol Petrol is cheap and a tankful goes far. Don't buy too much at a time – most firms expect you to take the car back empty.

Public transport Jersey has the second highest proportion of motor vehicles per head of population in the world behind Guernsey. Needless to say, there are jams in the busier parts of the island, but it's surprising how quickly traffic disperses on all those tiny lanes. If you don't care to drive, buses operate along the main roads, and you can always hire a bike. Jersey also has a splendid network of 'Green Lane' footpaths and coastal trails which take you through gorgeous scenery away from the cars and madding crowds. The tourist offices produce excellent, clear walks leaflets which avoid busy roads as far as possible. The cliff path on the north coast of Jersey takes you past the best of the island's scenery.

Jersey has a good bus system, though services are less frequent off season, in the evenings, and on Sundays. An Explorer ticket will allow you to hop on and off as much as you like. Most services radiate from St Helier bus station (☎ 01534 877772 for information and timetables). There are frequent services from the main towns to the airports.

Roads In general the road surfaces are good and road markings clear, but be aware that some roads are extremely narrow and have ditches either side – these are known as Green Lanes. They may have granite walls either side that can leave a nasty dent in the side of your car if driving recklessly – a good reason not to exceed the 25 km/h (15 mph) limit.

Rules of the road As in the UK, you drive on the left. A yellow line across a minor road means STOP. You must give way to traffic on the major road. Yellow arrows painted on the road warn of an approaching stop line, while a single yellow line along the side of the road means no parking at any time. A yellow box painted at a junction indicates a 'filter in turn' system. This simply means that all approach roads have equal priority, so you take it in turns with cars from other directions. Remember drink-driving penalties are strict.

Speed limits The maximum speed limit is 65 km/h (40 mph) on Jersey. In towns it is 40 km/h (25 mph) and on Green Lanes it is only 25 km/h (15 mph). If visiting Guernsey remember the maximum speed limit is 55 km/h (35 mph).

Taxis Taxi ranks can be found in St Helier and at the airport. Be aware that there are different tariffs applied for day and night hire and on public holidays. Extra charges may be charged for waiting time.

HEALTH MATTERS

All doctors, dentists and opticians operate private practices on Jersey but British visitors enjoy free medical treatment while they are on the islands. Not all costs are covered, and you are strongly advised to take out health insurance. Urgent dental problems, such as a sudden abscess, may be treated as medical emergencies. There is no need to take any forms with you, such as an EHIC medical card (which replaced the E111) but you do need to provide photographic proof of identity and UK citizenship to obtain treatment (for example a driving licence). Prescription charges are much lower than in the UK, but do take with you any medicines you need on a regular basis.

Health hazards Note that, with around 2,000 hours of sunshine a year, it is easy to get sunburned on Jersey. Despite a sea breeze, the air is clear and the ultra-violet is strong so you will need high factor sun protection.

Clinics The General Hospital in Gloucester Street, St Helier, runs a free morning clinic. ☎ 01534 725241 ◷ Mon–Sat (Mar–Sept); Mon, Wed & Fri only (Oct–Feb)

MEDIA

All the usual British publications, radio and TV stations are available on Jersey, as well as local media.

OPENING HOURS

Opening hours are generally the same as they are in Britain, but far fewer shops open on Sunday, except those in or near tourist attractions, and the odd grocery store.

PERSONAL COMFORT & SECURITY

Crime prevention Happily, crime is rare in Jersey, especially personal violence or street theft. Even so, take the usual precautionary measures:

for example, even if the islanders themselves don't always lock their doors, it makes sense for visitors to do so. Don't leave temptation in anyone's way and you are unlikely to suffer any losses. Take care of your personal property as you would at home.

Lost property Report any loss or theft to your holiday representative or hotel staff. Notify your bank or credit card company if you lose your cheque book or credit cards. If an insurance claim is to be made you must report a theft within 24 hours to the police. The lost property office in Jersey (☏ 01534 612305) may be able to help you.

POST OFFICES

The main post office is in Broad Street, St Helier, with a network of sub-post offices dotted around the island. Jersey mail must carry Jersey stamps, and you must use the correct stamps on any post mailed from Jersey. Pillar boxes are red. The central post offices and museums in Jersey have interesting displays of local stamps, which illustrate many aspects of island life and history.

PUBLIC TOILETS

Few destinations can match Jersey for their generous provision of free, clean, unvandalised public conveniences, many suitable for visitors with disabilities.

TIME DIFFERENCES

There is no time difference between Jersey and the UK, which uses Greenwich Mean Time (GMT). The clocks go forward in April and back in October.

TRAVELLERS WITH DISABILITIES

Jersey has taken great steps to help the disabled enjoy it to the full, such as on buses, at ferry terminals and the airport. However, there are not many hire cars and taxis that are suitably adapted for people with disabilities, and there are still some sights that will be difficult to get

TELEPHONES
Jersey's telecom service is modern, efficient and relatively inexpensive. Public call boxes (mostly yellow) are widespread, and use the same dialling codes as the UK. Most require phonecards, available from newsagents and post offices.

TELEPHONING JERSEY
Jersey's dialling code from the UK is 01534.

round, although many – along with hotels and restaurants – have made suitably helpful changes. For further information check the tourist office website or with:

RADAR The principal UK forum and pressure group for people with disabilities Ⓦ 12 City Forum, 250 City Road, London EC1V 8AF ❶ (020) 7250 3222 Ⓦ www.radar.org.uk

WEIGHTS & MEASUREMENTS
Jersey operates the same metric system as in the UK.

A

accommodation 110–11
adventure park 103
air travel 112, 115–16, 117
Alderney 76–81, 104

B

baggage allowances and packing
    tips 114–15
Battle of Flowers Museum 38
beaches 10, 14, 50–3, 103, 117
Beaucette Marina 64
birdwatching 40, 79
boat trips 78, 89
Bonne Nuit Bay 10, 52, 57
Bouley Bay 28, 52, 58
bowls 106
Brecqhou Island 92, 93
buses 121

C

car hire 115, 120
Channel Islands 8, 10–11
children 102–3, 117–18
climate 114
Corbière Point 42
Corbière Walk 45
credit and debit cards 113, 119
crime 122–3
customs allowances 116

D

Devil's Hole 33, 57
disabilities, travellers with 123–4
driving 54–8, 113, 115, 120, 121
Durrell Wildlife Conservation Trust
    (Jersey Zoo) 15, 28, 102

E

eating out 96–9
    see also individual locations
electricity 119
Elizabeth Castle 15, 18, 102, 103
emergencies 119, 122
Eric Young Orchid Foundation 29

F

ferry services 8, 120
festivals and events 104
Fisherman's Chapel 15, 43
fishing 106
food and drink 96–9
Fort Regent 18, 20, 102, 106
freesia glasshouses 65

G

German Occupation Museum
    71–2
German Underground Hospital 72
Glass Church 15, 46
gold and silversmiths 47–8, 67, 101
golf 106
Gorey Village 15, 29
Grève de Lecq 10, 33, 34, 38, 52, 56
Grosnez Castle 40, 54
Grouville 10, 24–7, 53
Guernsey 11, 59–75

H

Hamptonne Country Life Museum
    14, 46, 47, 102
Hauteville House 59, 61
Herm 82–6
history 10–13
horse riding 106–7

I

inoculations 112
insurance 113–14

J

Jersey Museum 12, 15, 20, 102
Jersey War Tunnels 13, 14, 46, 48

K

Kempt Tower 38, 39

L

La Gran'mère di Chimquière 72, 73
La Hougue Bie 24, 102
La Mare Wine Estate 34, 35

La Valette Underground Military
    Museum 61
Langtry, Lillie 12, 46
lavender farm 43
Le Moulin de Quétivel 43
Les Mielles 39
lighthouses 45, 79
Lihou Island 68
L'Ile Agois 34
The Living Legend 41, 43
lost property 123

M

Maritime Museum 20–1, 102
medical treatment 122
money 113, 119
Mont Orgueil Castle 15, 30, 102
Mont St Michel 94
motor sports 107

N

Neolithic sites 24, 34, 64, 84
nightlife *see* individual locations
North Coast Visitor Centre 34, 35

O

Occupation Tapestry 13, 21
opening hours 122
Ouaisné Common 50

P

Pallot Heritage Steam Museum 30
passports 113
pearls 38–9, 101
Plémont Bay 38, 52, 54
Plémont Point 40
post offices 123
potteries 25, 38, 72, 74

Q

Queen's Valley Reservoir 31

R

Rozel Bay 10, 28, 52, 58

S

sailing 108
St Aubin 42, 45, 46, 50
St Brelade's Bay 8, 10, 41–4, 50
St Catherine's Bay 28, 52, 58
St Clement 10, 24–7, 53
St Helier 8, 10, 13, 18–23, 101
St John 10, 33–6
St Lawrence 10, 46-8
St Malo 8, 94
St Martin 10, 28–32
St Mary 10, 33–6
St Ouen 10, 37–40, 51, 54
St Peter 10, 41–4
St Peter Port 59–63
St Saviour 10, 46–8
St Saviour's Church 12, 15, 46
Samarès Manor 14, 26
Sark 11, 87–94
Saumarez Park & Folk Museum
    65–6
Sausmarez Manor 74
Shell Garden 103
Shipwreck Museum 68
shopping 100–1
Sorel Point 57
sports and activities 106–8
Strawberry Farm 68
sun safety 112, 122

T

taxis 122
Telephone Museum 66
telephones 119, 124
time differences 123
toilets 123
tourist information 119
Trinity 10, 28–32

W

watersports 64, 108
Wolf's Caves 33
woodcarving studio 68–9

FIND THE LATEST HOTSPOT

Get more from your holiday and find out the best restaurants, bars, beaches and family-friendly attractions from our handy pocket guides. Our wide range covers up to 45 destinations:

Algarve
Bali
Bulgaria
Corfu
Corsica
Costa Blanca
Costa Brava & Costa Dorada
Costa del Sol & Costa de Almeria
Côte D'Azur
Crete
Croatia
Cuba
Cyprus
Dominican Republic
Egypt
Fuerteventura
Gibraltar
Goa
Gran Canaria
Guernsey
Ibiza
Ionian Islands
Jamaica

Jersey
Lanzarote
Madeira
Mallorca
Malta
Menorca
Mexico
Morocco
Neapolitan Riviera
Orlando
Rhodes & Kos
Santorini
Sardinia
Sicily
Sri Lanka
Tenerife
Thailand
Tunisia
Turkey –
    Aegean Coast
    Lycian Coast
    Mediterranean Coast

Available from all good bookshops, your local Thomas Cook travel store or browse and buy on-line at www.thomascookpublishing.com

Thomas Cook Publishing

ACKNOWLEDGEMENTS

We would like to thank all the photographers, picture libraries and organisations for the loan of the photographs reproduced in this book, to whom copyright in the photograph belongs:

Anwer Bati (pages 1, 10, 14–15, 26, 29, 30, 34, 36, 49, 65, 73, 89, 90, 98, 103, 109); J. Allen Cash (page 42); Jersey Tourism (pages 5, 9, 12, 17, 20, 25, 33, 37, 39, 41, 47, 51, 55, 95, 97, 100, 105, 107, 118); VisitGuernsey (pages 56, 69, 75, 78, 79, 81, 84, 85, 93).

Project editor: Catherine Burch
Layout: Donna Pedley
Proofreader: Penny Isaac
Indexer: Marie Lorimer

Send your thoughts to
books@thomascook.com

- Found a beach bar, peaceful stretch of sand or must-see sight that we don't feature?

- Like to tip us off about any information that needs a little updating?

- Want to tell us what you love about this handy little guidebook and more importantly how we can make it even handier?

Then here's your chance to tell all! Send us ideas, discoveries and recommendations today and then look out for your valuable input in the next edition of this title.

Send an email to the above address or write to:
HotSpots Project Editor, Thomas Cook Publishing, PO Box 227, Coningsby Road, Peterborough PE3 8SB, UK